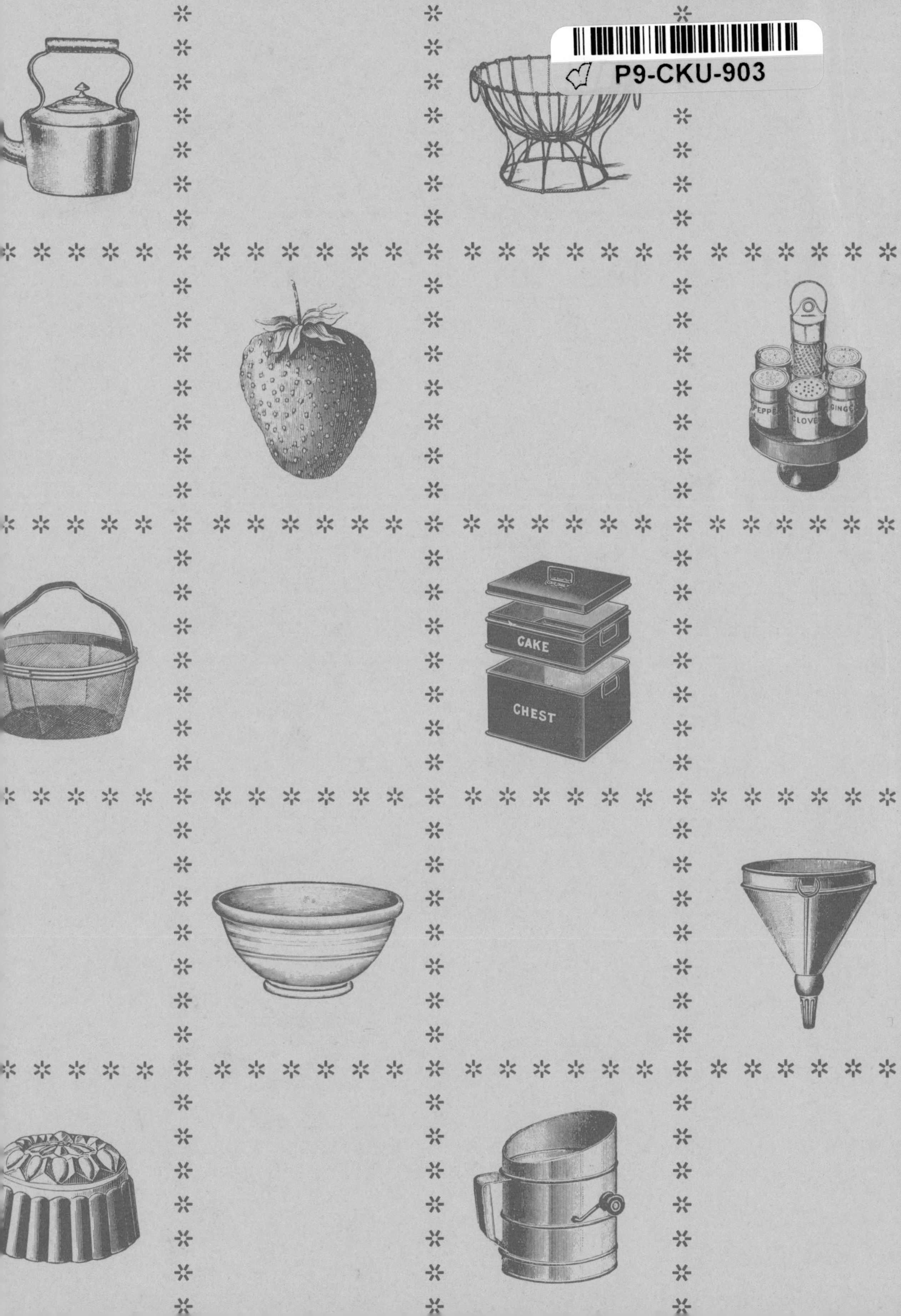
CLOVE
CAKE
CHEST

Southern Living.

The
SOUTHERN
HERITAGE
COOKBOOK
LIBRARY

The SOUTHERN HERITAGE
Vegetables
COOKBOOK

OXMOOR HOUSE
Birmingham, Alabama

Southern Living ®

The Southern Heritage Cookbook Library

Copyright 1983 by Oxmoor House, Inc.
Book Division of Southern Progress Corporation
P.O. Box 2262, Birmingham, Alabama 35201

Southern Living® is a federally registered trademark belonging to
Southern Living, Inc.

Library of Congress Catalog Number: 83-060429
ISBN: 0-8487-0605-6

Manufactured in the United States of America

The Southern Heritage VEGETABLES Cookbook

Manager, Editorial Projects: Ann H. Harvey
Southern Living® *Foods Editor*: Jean W. Liles
Production Editor: Joan E. Denman
Foods Editor: Katherine M. Eakin
Director, Test Kitchen: Laura N. Nestelroad
Test Kitchen Home Economists: Pattie B. Booker, Kay E. Clarke,
   Marilyn Hannan, Elizabeth J. Taliaferro
Production Manager: Jerry R. Higdon
Copy Editor: Melinda E. West
Editorial Assistant: Karen P. Traccarella
Food Photographer: Jim Bathie
Food Stylist: Sara Jane Ball
Layout Designer: Christian von Rosenvinge
Mechanical Artist: Faith Nance
Research Assistant: Janice Randall

Special Consultants

Art Director: Irwin Glusker
Heritage Consultant: Meryle Evans
Foods Writer: Lillian B. Marshall
Food and Recipe Consultants: Marilyn Wyrick Ingram,
   Audrey P. Stehle

Cover (clockwise from front): Seasoned Baked Tomatoes (page 119),
Succotash (page 127), and Green Beans and New Potatoes (page 23).
Photograph by Jim Bathie.

CONTENTS

INTRODUCTION

If an eccentric aunt issued an invitation to dinner, promising Stuffed Thistles, Casserole of Nightshades, Lilies in Hollandaise, and Morning Glory Pie, which way would you run? Unless you come from a long line of witches, you'll make haste to accept, send her an extravagant centerpiece, and be on time for the first course. What she means, naturally, is that her garden is overflowing with artichokes, eggplant, tomatoes, potatoes, asparagus, leeks, onions, and sweet potatoes.

These vegetables by their family names only seem strange; they are the same Southern favorites that inspired William Byrd to call Virginia the "Garden of Eden." Byrd wrote of this Eden in his *Natural History of Virginia*, 1737, singing praises to its fruits, including two dozen kinds of apples and the vegetables that had long been cultivated there: artichokes, "beautiful cauliflower . . . very large and long asparagus of splendid flavor . . . watermelons and fragrant melons," as well as the pumpkins, squashes, and cucumbers that grew so easily in the rich fields.

Our vegetable gardens are lessons in history and geography. Think of the peregrinations of the Peruvian potato and the Mexican tomato to Europe and full circle back to our side of the Atlantic. Vegetables preserved in brine were eaten by the builders of the Great Wall of China, and peas sustained the labor force on the Great Pyramids. We may smile to think of the "mad apple" eggplant and the "love apple" tomato being grown for centuries for their beauty alone, and the potato merely for its flower.

So play it smart; say "Yes, thank you!" to Auntie. Go on over and eat all those esculent lilies and yummy thistles before her garden shuts down for the season. Here is a hint: be early and watch how a Southern cook seasons and sauces the vegetables—a magic touch that sets her vegetables apart from those outside the region.

Then, armed with this book filled with vegetable recipes, you can achieve the same creative results as Auntie. Each vegetable section begins with the basic methods of preparing, cooking, and serving that particular "fruit of the earth"; a glossary of cooking terms explains both old and new cooking techniques; and the "Final Touches" chapter is just that—here you can find recipes for all the suggested sauces and accompaniments for vegetables. Now, on to vegetable cookery!

ARTICHOKES

HOW TO PREPARE FRESH ARTICHOKES

4 artichokes
1 lemon

To Clean: Wash by plunging up and down in cold water. Cut off stem end; cut off ½-inch straight across top. Discard loose bottom leaves. With scissors, trim away one-fourth of each outer leaf. Drop into acidulated water (juice of 1 lemon to 1 quart of water), or rub tops and edges of leaves with a lemon wedge, to prevent discoloration.

To Boil: Place artichokes in 2 inches of water in a large Dutch oven. Bring to a boil. Cover and reduce heat; simmer 30 minutes. Cool slightly.

To Serve: Spread leaves apart; pull out center leaves, and scrape out the fuzzy thistle center (choke) with a spoon; discard choke. Serve with a sauce to the side or placed in the cavity of cleaned artichoke. Yield: 4 servings.

Serving Suggestions: Artichokes may be served warm or chilled as an appetizer or salad with any of the following: Drawn Butter, French Dressing, Homemade Mayonnaise, Horseradish Sauce, Lemon-Butter Sauce, Mustard Dip Sauce, or any hollandaise sauce.

For a decorative appetizer, use the artichoke as a container for sauce.

STUFFED ARTICHOKES

2 artichokes, cleaned and boiled
¾ cup mayonnaise
3 hard-cooked eggs, finely chopped
Lettuce leaves

Cool artichokes slightly. Spread leaves apart; pull out center leaves, and scrape out fuzzy thistle center (choke) with a spoon. Discard. After choke has been completely removed, scrape the artichoke heart with a spoon to remove as much pulp as possible; reserve pulp. (Be careful not to separate outer leaves from base of artichoke.) Set artichokes aside.

Finely chop reserved pulp; combine with mayonnaise and chopped egg, mixing well. Spoon mixture into center of each artichoke; chill. Place stuffed artichokes upright on lettuce leaves before serving. Yield: 2 servings.

ARTICHOKE HEARTS

8 artichokes, cleaned and
  boiled

Pull away the leaf sections of
each cooked artichoke, starting
from the outside and working
toward the center. Discard
leaves. Scrape out the fuzzy
thistle center (choke) with a
spoon, leaving the heart. Trim
rough edges from bottom of
each heart.

Serve artichoke hearts warm
or chilled with sauce. Yield: 4
servings.

Serving Suggestions: Artichoke hearts may be served with
Horseradish Sauce or any hollandaise sauce, in salads, or as a
base for stuffings.

CREAMED ARTICHOKE HEARTS

8 artichokes, cleaned and
  boiled
1 tablespoon butter or
  margarine
1 tablespoon all-purpose flour
1 cup whipping cream
2½ tablespoons sherry
⅛ teaspoon salt
⅛ teaspoon pepper
Dash of hot sauce

Pull away the leaf sections of
each cooked artichoke, starting
from the outside and working
toward the center. Scrape the
base of each leaf section with a
knife; reserve pulp and set
aside. Discard leaves. Scrape
out the fuzzy thistle center
(choke) with a spoon, leaving
the heart. Trim rough edges
from bottom of heart. Cut heart
in quarters and set aside.

Melt butter in a heavy saucepan over low heat; add flour,
and stir until smooth. Cook 1
minute, stirring constantly.
Gradually add whipping cream;
cook over medium heat, stirring
constantly, until thickened and
bubbly. Add sherry, salt, pepper, and hot sauce, mixing well.
Add reserved artichoke pulp and
hearts; heat thoroughly. Serve
hot. Yield: 4 servings.

Spiced Jerusalem Artichokes

JERUSALEM ARTICHOKES

HOW TO PREPARE FRESH JERUSALEM ARTICHOKES

1½ pounds Jerusalem
  artichokes

To Clean: Wash thoroughly;
peel and rinse well. Artichokes
may be left whole, cut into thin
slices, or cubed, as directed in
recipe. Drop into lightly acidulated water (juice of 1 lemon to 1
quart of water); drain.

To Boil: Cook artichokes in
boiling salted water to cover 10
minutes or until tender. Drain;
cool. Yield: 4 servings.

Other Cooking Methods: Parboil, then batter and deep-fry;
sauté.

Serving Suggestions: Jerusalem artichokes may be served
with any of the following: Drawn
Butter, Horseradish Sauce,
Lemon-Butter Sauce, or any
hollandaise or white sauce.
They may be thinly sliced and
served raw in salads or as a sub-
stitute for water chestnuts.

SPICED JERUSALEM ARTICHOKES

1½ pounds Jerusalem
  artichokes, cleaned and
  boiled
½ clove garlic, minced
2 tablespoons vegetable oil
¼ cup plus 2 tablespoons
  vinegar
2 tablespoons water
1 tablespoon sugar
½ teaspoon dry mustard
½ teaspoon salt

Cut artichokes into ¼-inch
slices. Sauté artichokes and
garlic in oil about 10 minutes,
stirring frequently. Combine remaining ingredients; pour over
artichokes, and simmer about 5
minutes. Serve hot or cold.
Yield: 4 servings.

ASPARAGUS

HOW TO PREPARE FRESH ASPARAGUS

1 pound fresh asparagus spears

To Clean: Wash carefully under running water to flush out sand from tips. Find the point at the end of each stalk where it breaks easily and snap off. Line up tips, and cut off ends even with broken stalk. If desired, remove scales with a vegetable peeler.

To Steam: Tie asparagus into a bundle with kitchen string. Stand bundle, tips up, in bottom of double boiler. Add boiling water to fill pan half full. Cover with top of double boiler, turned upside down, for a lid. Simmer 6 minutes for use in salads and 12 minutes or until crisp-tender to serve hot. Drain and refresh quickly by running asparagus under cold water to retain color. Chill for use in salads. To serve hot, place in a serving bowl, and snip string. Yield: 4 servings.

To Boil: Fill a saucepan three-fourths full of water; add salt and bring to a boil. Place asparagus in boiling water; cover until water returns to a boil. Uncover, reduce heat, and simmer 12 minutes or until a knife point will easily pierce the spears. Drain well. Serve immediately. Yield: 4 servings.

Other Cooking Methods: Bake; deep-fry; stir-fry.

Serving Suggestions: Asparagus may be served over toast points and topped with Drawn Butter or served with Cheese Sauce, Grandma Flexner's Asparagus Sauce, Horseradish Sauce, or any hollandaise sauce.

Vegetables *is part of Sweetie Ladd's* Cries of Ft. Worth, *a series of watercolors capturing a facet of Ft. Worth at the turn of the century.*

Courtesy of Hall Galleries, Ft. Worth

FRESH ASPARAGUS IN BACON RINGS

4 slices bacon
1 pound fresh asparagus
  spears, cleaned and cooked
2 tablespoons butter or
  margarine, melted
Salt and pepper to taste

Invert a large muffin pan, and place bacon slices around the outside of 4 individual muffin cups. Secure ends of bacon with wooden picks.

Place inverted muffin pan with bacon on upper shelf of oven. Bake at 350° for 15 minutes or until bacon is crisp. Remove from oven, and carefully remove bacon rings from muffin cups. Remove wooden picks.

Gently slide 5 to 6 cooked asparagus spears inside each bacon ring. Pour a small amount of melted butter over each serving, and season with salt and pepper. Serve immediately. Yield: 4 servings.

ASPARAGUS WITH MUSHROOMS AND CREAM SAUCE

1 pound large fresh
  mushrooms
¼ cup plus 1 tablespoon
  butter, divided
Chopped fresh parsley
3 tablespoons all-purpose
  flour
1 cup whipping cream
½ cup milk
¼ teaspoon salt
¼ teaspoon white pepper
2 pounds fresh asparagus
  spears, cleaned and cooked
2 tablespoons grated
  Parmesan cheese

Clean mushrooms with damp paper towels or a mushroom brush. Remove stems and chop. Sauté mushroom caps and stems in 2 tablespoons butter. Remove from heat; drain. Fill each cap with parsley. Set stems and caps aside.

Melt remaining butter in a heavy saucepan over low heat; add flour, stirring until smooth.

Asparagus served with mushrooms and cream sauce.

Cook 1 minute, stirring constantly. Gradually add whipping cream and milk; cook over medium heat, stirring constantly, until mixture is thickened and bubbly. Add salt, pepper, and reserved mushroom stems.

Arrange cooked asparagus spears and mushroom caps on an ovenproof serving dish. Pour sauce over asparagus. Sprinkle with cheese. Place under broiler 3 minutes or until lightly browned. Yield: 8 servings.

For fifty years, Martha Washington used a manuscript cookbook containing recipes for assorted vegetables grown at Mt. Vernon. Included were asparagus, artichokes, cucumbers, carrots, turnips, parsnips, and skirrets (a sweet edible turber).

ASPARAGUS AND PEAS WITH EGG SAUCE

1 pound fresh asparagus spears, cleaned and cut into 1-inch pieces
1 (10-ounce) package frozen green peas
2 tablespoons butter or margarine
2 tablespoons all-purpose flour
2 cups milk
½ teaspoon salt
¼ teaspoon pepper
2 hard-cooked eggs, chopped
6 slices bread, toasted and lightly buttered
Dried whole dillweed

Cook asparagus, covered, in a small amount of boiling salted water 6 minutes or until crisp-tender. Drain well; set aside.

Cook peas according to package directions. Drain well and set aside.

Melt butter in a heavy saucepan over low heat; add flour, stirring until smooth. Cook 1 minute, stirring constantly. Gradually add milk; cook over medium heat, stirring constantly, until thickened and bubbly. Add salt, pepper, and chopped eggs.

Combine asparagus and peas. Spoon vegetables evenly onto toast slices; top with cream sauce. Sprinkle with dillweed. Yield: 6 servings.

MARION HARLAND'S AMBUSHED ASPARAGUS

6 hard rolls
¼ cup butter or margarine, melted
1 pound fresh asparagus spears, cleaned and cut into 1½-inch pieces
¼ cup butter or margarine
¼ cup all-purpose flour
2 cups milk
¼ teaspoon salt
¼ teaspoon pepper
Dash of ground nutmeg
Paprika

Cut a ¾-inch slice from top of each roll; scoop out center, leaving a ½-inch shell. Brush inside of each roll with melted butter; bake roll bottoms and tops at 300° for 30 minutes or until rolls are crisp.

Cook asparagus, covered, in a small amount of boiling salted water 6 minutes or until crisp-tender. Drain well; set aside.

Melt ¼ cup butter in a heavy saucepan over low heat; blend in flour and cook 1 minute, stirring constantly. Gradually add milk; cook over medium heat, stirring constantly, until smooth and thickened. Stir in salt, pepper, and nutmeg. Add cooked asparagus, stirring well. Fill bottom halves of rolls with asparagus mixture; sprinkle with paprika. Cover with tops of rolls. Yield: 6 servings.

ASPARAGUS VINAIGRETTE

1 pound fresh asparagus spears, cleaned and cooked
¼ cup butter or margarine, melted
⅓ cup lemon juice
1 teaspoon salt
¼ teaspoon paprika
Dash of pepper
1 tablespoon chopped pimiento
1 tablespoon chopped dill pickle
1 tablespoon chopped green pepper
1 tablespoon chopped onion
1 tablespoon chopped fresh parsley
2 hard-cooked eggs

Place warm asparagus spears on a serving dish.

Combine remaining ingredients, except eggs, in a medium saucepan. Cook over medium heat 2 minutes, stirring frequently. Pour sauce over asparagus.

Finely chop egg yolks; reserve whites for use in other recipes. Sprinkle yolks over asparagus and serve. Yield: 4 servings.

BAKED FRESH ASPARAGUS

1½ pounds fresh asparagus spears, cleaned
½ teaspoon salt
Dash of pepper
3 tablespoons butter or margarine

Place cleaned whole asparagus spears in a 12- x 8- x 2-inch baking dish. Sprinkle with salt and pepper; dot with butter. Cover, and bake asparagus at 300° for 30 minutes. Yield: 6 servings.

Serving Suggestions: Baked Fresh Asparagus may be served with Asparagus White Sauce, Cheese Sauce, Drawn Butter, Hollandaise Sauce Supreme, or any sour cream sauce.

Gardening on the grounds of Winthrop College in Rock Hill, South Carolina, c.1813.

ASPARAGUS MERINGUE

1 pound fresh asparagus
  spears, cleaned and cut
  into ¾-inch pieces
¼ cup butter or margarine
¼ cup all-purpose flour
3 eggs, separated
2 cups milk
½ cup (2 ounces) shredded
  sharp Cheddar cheese
¼ teaspoon salt
¼ teaspoon pepper
⅛ teaspoon cream of
  tartar

Cook asparagus, covered, in a small amount of boiling salted water 6 minutes or until crisp-tender; drain well. Arrange asparagus evenly in a 1½-quart casserole; set aside.

Melt butter in a heavy sauce-pan over low heat; add flour, stirring until smooth. Cook 1 minute, stirring constantly. Beat egg yolks; combine with milk, stirring well. Gradually add milk mixture to flour mixture, stirring constantly. Cook over medium heat, stirring constantly, until sauce is thickened and bubbly. Add cheese, salt, and pepper; stir until cheese melts. Pour cheese sauce over asparagus.

Combine egg whites (at room temperature) and cream of tartar; beat until stiff peaks form. Spread meringue over cheese sauce, sealing to edge of casserole. Bake at 400° for 8 to 10 minutes or until meringue is lightly browned. Serve immediately. Yield: 6 servings.

FRIED FRESH ASPARAGUS

1 pound fresh asparagus
  spears, cleaned
2 eggs, beaten
1½ cups cracker crumbs
Vegetable oil

Snap off tough ends of asparagus, leaving about a 4-inch tip; discard ends. Dip asparagus tips in egg; dredge in crumbs. Repeat procedure for thicker coating.

Deep-fry asparagus in hot oil (375°) for 5 minutes or until golden brown. Drain well on paper towels. Yield: 4 servings.

Serving Suggestion: Fried Fresh Asparagus may be served as an appetizer with Mustard Dip Sauce.

BAKED ASPARAGUS PATTIES

1 tablespoon butter or margarine
1½ tablespoons all-purpose flour
1 cup milk
1 egg yolk
½ teaspoon salt
Pinch of red pepper
1 teaspoon onion juice
1 (15-ounce) can asparagus spears, drained and cut into ½-inch pieces
2 cups fine, dry breadcrumbs

Melt butter in a heavy saucepan over low heat; add flour, stirring until smooth. Cook 1 minute, stirring constantly. Combine milk and egg yolk, stirring well; gradually add to flour mixture. Cook over medium heat, stirring constantly, until thickened and bubbly. Stir in salt, pepper, onion juice, and asparagus pieces; chill mixture thoroughly.

Shape into patties, using about ¼ cup mixture for each. Roll patties in breadcrumbs, and place on an ungreased baking sheet. Bake at 350° for 20 minutes or until tops are golden brown. Turn and bake an additional 5 minutes. Yield: 6 to 8 servings.

SCALLOPED ASPARAGUS WITH ALMONDS

3 tablespoons butter or margarine
3 tablespoons all-purpose flour
1½ cups milk
1 teaspoon salt
½ teaspoon pepper
1 (10½-ounce) can asparagus spears, drained
1 cup chopped blanched almonds
1 cup (4 ounces) shredded sharp Cheddar cheese
3 tablespoons fine, dry breadcrumbs

Melt butter in a heavy saucepan over low heat; add flour, stirring until smooth. Cook 1 minute, stirring constantly. Gradually add milk; cook over medium heat, stirring constantly, until mixture is thickened and bubbly. Add salt and pepper; set aside.

Layer half of the asparagus, cream sauce, almonds, cheese, and breadcrumbs in a lightly greased 1-quart casserole; repeat procedure with remaining ingredients. Bake at 350° for 20 minutes or until lightly browned. Yield: 6 to 8 servings.

ASPARAGUS SOUFFLÉ

1 (10½-ounce) can asparagus spears, undrained
¼ cup butter or margarine
¼ cup all-purpose flour
1 cup milk
½ teaspoon salt
5 eggs, separated

Drain asparagus, reserving liquid. Finely chop asparagus. Combine asparagus and liquid to yield 1 cup, discarding any fibrous pieces. Set mixture aside.

Melt butter in top of a double boiler over boiling water; add flour, stirring until smooth. Cook 1 minute, stirring constantly. Gradually stir in milk; add asparagus mixture and salt. Cook over boiling water, stirring constantly, until mixture coats a metal spoon. Remove from heat.

Beat egg yolks. Add one-fourth of hot asparagus sauce to yolks, stirring well; return to hot mixture. Cook over boiling water, stirring constantly, until thickened and bubbly. Remove from heat and cool.

Beat egg whites (at room temperature) until stiff but not dry. Fold into asparagus mixture. Spoon into a greased 1½-quart soufflé dish. Bake at 325° for 1 hour or until golden brown. Yield: 4 to 6 servings.

Asparagus, most delicious member of the lily-of-the-valley family, is native to the eastern Mediterranean lands, where it continues to grow wild. From Greece to Rome to England it came, and colonists brought roots for starting the vegetable in America. It is colloquially known as "sparrow grass"; tradesmen just call it "grass." Europeans prefer to bleach it white by covering it when the tips show.

BEANS

HOW TO PREPARE DRIED BEANS

2 cups dried beans (lima, navy, or pinto)
Salt and pepper
4½ cups water

Regular Soak: Sort and wash beans; place in a Dutch oven or a large saucepan. Cover with water 2 inches above beans; let soak overnight. Drain beans well before cooking.

Quick Soak: Sort and wash beans; place in a Dutch oven. Cover with water 2 inches above beans; bring to a boil and cook 5 minutes. Remove from heat; let stand 1 hour. Drain well.

To Simmer: Combine soaked beans, seasoning, and water in a Dutch oven; bring to a boil. Reduce heat; cover and simmer 2½ hours or until beans are tender. Yield: 6 servings.

Other Cooking Methods: Bake after soaking.

Serving Suggestions: Lima and navy beans may be served with catsup, Drawn Butter, Lemon-Butter Sauce, or any sour cream sauce; pinto beans may be served with Basil Vinegar, Hot Pepper Sauce, or Mason County Relish.

DRIED LIMA BEANS WITH SAUSAGE

1 (16-ounce) package dried lima beans, soaked and drained
10 pork sausage links
¼ cup all-purpose flour
1¼ cups evaporated milk
2 tablespoons chopped pimiento
½ teaspoon salt
Minced fresh parsley

Place beans in a large saucepan; cover with water 3 inches above beans. Cover and bring to a boil; reduce heat, and simmer 2½ hours or until beans are tender. Drain beans, reserving 1 cup cooking liquid. Set liquid aside. Transfer beans to a serving dish; keep warm.

Cook sausage in a large skillet until browned. Remove sausage, and cut each link into thirds; set aside. Reserve ¼ cup drippings in skillet.

Add flour to drippings; stir until smooth. Cook 1 minute, stirring constantly. Gradually add milk and reserved liquid; cook over medium heat, stirring constantly, until thickened and bubbly. Add pimiento and salt.

Pour sauce over beans. Garnish with sausage and parsley. Yield: 6 to 8 servings.

Hearty wintertime supper: Dried Lima Beans with Sausage.

SOUTHERN-COOKED DRIED LIMA BEANS

2 cups dried lima beans, soaked and drained
4½ cups water
¼ pound salt pork, sliced
1 teaspoon salt
½ teaspoon pepper

Combine beans, water, salt pork, salt, and pepper in a large saucepan; bring to a boil. Reduce heat; cover and simmer 2½ hours or until beans are tender. Yield: 6 servings.

CREOLE LIMA BEANS

1½ cups dried lima beans, soaked and drained
1 cup chopped onion
2 tablespoons chopped green pepper
2 tablespoons butter or margarine
1 tablespoon plus 1½ teaspoons all-purpose flour
1 (14½-ounce) can stewed tomatoes, undrained
⅓ cup water
1 teaspoon sugar
½ teaspoon salt

Place beans in a large saucepan; cover with water 3 inches above beans. Cover and bring to a boil; reduce heat and simmer 2 hours or until beans are tender. Set aside.

Sauté onion and green pepper in butter in a large skillet until tender; add flour, stirring until well blended. Cook 1 minute, stirring constantly. Gradually add tomatoes and water; cook over medium heat, stirring constantly, until thickened and bubbly. Add sugar and salt; pour over beans, and mix well. Cook an additional 20 minutes, stirring frequently. Yield: 4 to 6 servings.

BAKED NAVY BEANS

9 slices bacon, divided
2 medium onions, chopped
3 (14½-ounce) cans stewed tomatoes, undrained
¼ cup plus 2 tablespoons molasses
2 teaspoons salt
2 teaspoons chili powder
1 teaspoon pepper
1 teaspoon prepared mustard
1 (16-ounce) package dried navy beans, cooked

Cook 5 slices of bacon in a large skillet until crisp. Remove bacon, reserving the drippings in skillet. Crumble bacon and set aside.

Sauté onion in reserved drippings until tender. Add tomatoes, molasses, salt, chili powder, pepper, mustard, and crumbled bacon; cook over medium heat 35 minutes. Combine tomato mixture and beans, stirring gently.

Spoon beans into a lightly greased 13- x 9- x 2-inch baking dish; top with remaining bacon slices. Bake at 350° for 1 hour. Serve warm in baking dish. Yield: 10 to 12 servings.

"I have always heard that most vegetables and meat should have salt added after they are done or almost done. This keeps the salt from drawing out the water . . . or some such thing. On the other hand, things like dumplings, dried beans, and macaroni need some time for the salt to penetrate, and it should be added *during* the cooking time."

Heart-of-Texas Cookbook

SEASONED NAVY BEANS

1 (16-ounce) package dried navy beans, soaked and drained
1 teaspoon soda
1½ cups cubed salt pork
1½ cups chopped onion
2 cloves garlic, minced
1 teaspoon salt
½ teaspoon red pepper flakes
½ cup chopped fresh parsley

Combine beans and soda in a Dutch oven; add water to cover 2 inches above beans. Cover and bring to a boil. Reduce heat, and simmer 30 minutes. Drain and rinse beans well. Set aside.

Place salt pork in Dutch oven and cook until evenly browned; remove salt pork, reserving drippings. Sauté onion and garlic in reserved drippings until tender. Add beans, salt pork, salt, and red pepper flakes; cover with water and cook over low heat for 2 hours or until beans are tender, stirring occasionally. Garnish with parsley. Yield: 6 to 8 servings.

LEFTOVER NAVY BEANS

⅔ cup chopped onion
3 tablespoons bacon drippings
1⅓ cups cooked navy beans
1 (14½-ounce) can stewed tomatoes, undrained and chopped
Salt and pepper to taste

Sauté onion in bacon drippings in a large skillet until tender. Add beans; cook over low heat 2 minutes. Add tomatoes; continue to cook an additional 5 minutes, stirring frequently. Stir in salt and pepper to taste. Yield: 4 servings.

Seasoned Navy Beans: With a package of dried navies on the pantry shelf, a savory, but thrifty, main dish can be put together with ease.

CHUCKWAGON PINTO BEANS

1 (32-ounce) package dried pinto beans, soaked and drained
½ pound salt pork, cut into 1-inch cubes
1 tablespoon salt
½ teaspoon pepper
½ red pepper pod

Place prepared pinto beans in a large Dutch oven. Add salt pork cubes, salt, pepper, and red pepper pod. Add water to cover 3 inches above beans. Cover and bring water to a boil; reduce heat, and simmer for 3 hours or until beans are tender. Yield: 12 servings.

SEASONED PINTO BEANS

1 (32-ounce) package dried pinto beans, soaked and drained
1 pound salt pork, cubed
1 medium onion, chopped
½ teaspoon pepper
½ cup catsup (optional)

Combine beans, salt pork, and onion in a large Dutch oven; add water to cover 3 inches above beans. Bring to a boil; reduce heat. Cover and simmer 3 hours or until beans are tender. Stir in pepper; cook an additional 30 minutes, stirring occasionally. Stir in catsup before serving, if desired. Yield: 12 servings.

Frontiersmen wait for their campfire beans to cook.

FRIJOLES

1 (16-ounce) package dried pinto beans, soaked and drained
3½ tablespoons bacon drippings
4 green onions, chopped
2 cloves garlic, minced
½ teaspoon salt
½ teaspoon pepper
1 cup (4 ounces) shredded sharp Cheddar cheese

Place beans in a large Dutch oven with water to cover. Cover and bring to a boil; reduce heat, and simmer 2½ hours or until beans are tender.

Mash beans; add bacon drippings, and cook over medium heat 2 minutes, stirring constantly. Reduce heat; stir in onion, garlic, salt, and pepper. Cook, uncovered, over medium heat 30 minutes or until onion is tender, stirring occasionally. Sprinkle cheese over beans; simmer, without stirring, 5 minutes or until cheese melts. Yield: 6 to 8 servings.

LASYONE'S RED BEANS AND SAUSAGE

1 (16-ounce) package dried red kidney beans
10 cups water
½ cup vegetable oil
1 medium onion, chopped
1 medium-size green pepper, chopped
2 stalks celery, chopped
2 teaspoons salt
2 teaspoons sugar
1 teaspoon garlic powder
¾ teaspoon red pepper
½ teaspoon dried parsley flakes
1 cup ground smoked sausage
Hot cooked rice

Sort and wash beans. Combine beans and next 10 ingredients in a Dutch oven; bring to a boil. Reduce heat; cook, uncovered, over medium heat 1½ hours or until beans are tender.

Stir in sausage; cook 30 minutes. Serve over hot cooked rice. Yield: 6 to 8 servings.

BEAN AND SEED SEPARATOR.

Hundreds of bushels of refuse beans are taken to market annually, such as blighted or split beans, dirt and gravel stones, and the same freight paid on such as the best beans. They condemn the good beans and not near their value is realized.

We offer to those who raise and deal in produce, ADAMS' PATENT SEPARATOR, which will thoroughly cleanse beans from all dirt, bring out the split beans by themselves and separate the medium from the pea beans as well as the marrowfats; thus increasing the market value some 25 or 30 cents on the bushel, while the refuse saved at home is valuable for sheep and fowls.

Different grades of meshes are substituted that will separate oats from barley, wheat and buckwheat, and take out all foul seeds. They can be fitted to all Fan Mills. Also open meshes that will sort and take the sprouts off from potatoes.

Advertisement for patented bean-sorting equipment.

LOUISIANA RED BEANS AND RICE

3 cups dried red kidney beans
1 tablespoon vegetable oil
1 tablespoon all-purpose flour
1 medium onion, chopped
2 cloves garlic, minced
6 cups water
1 (½-pound) ham hock
1 sprig fresh parsley, minced
1 teaspoon salt
1 teaspoon red pepper
Hot cooked rice
6 medium-size green onions, chopped

Sort and wash beans. Set aside.

Combine oil and flour in a Dutch oven; cook over medium heat, stirring constantly, until roux is the color of a copper penny. Add onion and garlic; cook 5 minutes, stirring frequently.

Add 6 cups water, ham hock, parsley, salt, pepper, and beans; bring to a boil. Reduce heat; cover and simmer 1½ hours or until beans are tender and a thick gravy has formed. If necessary, add more water to prevent beans from sticking.

Mound rice in the middle of serving plates. Spoon beans around rice, and sprinkle with chopped green onion. Yield: 8 servings.

FRESH LIMA BEANS

HOW TO PREPARE FRESH LIMA BEANS

1 pound fresh lima or butter
  beans
2 cups water
½ teaspoon salt

To Shell and Clean: Break one tip, and "unzip" the string. Split the seam, preferably with a fingernail, and remove beans. Rinse in colander under cold running water.

To Simmer: Place beans, water, and salt in a medium saucepan; cover. Cook over medium heat 1 hour or until tender. Yield: 2 to 4 servings.

Serving Suggestions: Lima beans may be served with Drawn Butter or Lemon-Butter Sauce. Lima beans are also often served mixed with equal parts of hot cooked rice.

LIMA BEANS WITH ONION

2 cups shelled fresh lima
  beans
2 (¼-inch-thick) slices onion
½ cup boiling water
1 tablespoon finely chopped
  onion
2 tablespoons butter or
  margarine
⅓ cup chicken broth
1 tablespoon chopped fresh
  parsley
½ teaspoon salt
⅛ teaspoon pepper

Arrange beans and onion slices in steaming rack. Place over ½ cup boiling water; cover and steam 25 minutes or until crisp-tender. Remove from heat, and discard onion slices.

Sauté 1 tablespoon chopped onion in butter until tender; add beans and chicken broth. Cover and simmer 15 minutes. Add parsley, salt, and pepper; simmer an additional 2 minutes. Yield: 4 servings.

A vision of Jack and his beanstalk creates anticipation

A beam of light on the long-standing controversy about the difference, if any, between the butter bean and the lima bean: Yes, in Alabama (and Virginia and Kentucky), there is a butter bean; it is just that it is sometimes classified as a lima. Both are tropical American annuals. But the butter bean (which may also be found in the dictionary under "sieva bean") grows on a bush or on a weakly vining plant. The bean is small and may be variegated in color; it is hardly known outside the South.

Whereas the lima, named for Peru's capital, grows in bush or tall form and yields large, flat green or white seeds. It is grown in nearly all parts of the United States. The green ones, when picked before they are fully matured, are what Southerners call baby limas. Butter beans are not as large as full-grown lima beans and, in the opinion of some die-hards, are much more flavorful.

LIMA BEANS IN CREAM

2 cups shelled fresh lima
  beans
¾ cup half-and-half
1 tablespoon butter or
  margarine
¼ teaspoon salt
⅛ teaspoon pepper

Place lima beans in a steaming rack; place over boiling water and steam 20 minutes or until tender.

Combine beans, half-and-half, butter, salt, and pepper in a saucepan. Cook over low heat 5 minutes or until thoroughly heated. Yield: 4 servings.

SPECIAL BUTTER BEANS

6 cups shelled fresh butter
  beans
1 teaspoon salt
1 medium-size green pepper,
  chopped
¼ pound salt pork, sliced

Place beans with water to cover in a Dutch oven. Add salt, green pepper, and salt pork; bring to a boil. Reduce heat and cook, uncovered, over low heat 50 minutes or until beans are tender. Yield: 8 servings.

SOUTHERN-COOKED BUTTER BEANS

2 cups shelled fresh butter
  beans
2 cups water
2 tablespoons butter or
  margarine
1 tablespoon bacon drippings
½ teaspoon salt

Combine all ingredients in a saucepan; cover. Cook over medium heat 45 minutes or until tender. Yield: 2 to 3 servings.

GREEN BEANS

HOW TO PREPARE FRESH GREEN BEANS

2 pounds fresh green beans
¼ pound ham hock
1 teaspoon salt

To Snap: Do not wash beans before storing in refrigerator. When ready to use, break first one tip and then the other. Break into 1½-inch lengths. Wash in cold water.

Note: Some varieties of green beans have strings which should be removed before snapping. After breaking the tips, use them to "unzip" the strings.

To Simmer: Place beans and cold water to cover in a saucepan; let stand for 10 minutes. Add ham hock and bring water to a boil. Reduce heat and simmer, uncovered, 1 hour and 15 minutes or until beans are tender. For a real "down-home" flavor, cook beans an additional 2 hours. Yield: 8 servings.

Serving Suggestions: Green beans may be served with Almond Butter, Basil Vinegar, Chive Blossom Vinegar, Dill Sauce, or French Dressing.

GREEN BEANS WITH SALT PORK

½ pound salt pork, cut into
  ½-inch cubes
2 large onions, chopped
1 clove garlic, minced
2 pounds fresh green beans,
  snapped
Salt to taste

Cook salt pork in a large Dutch oven over medium heat, stirring frequently, until crisp and browned. Add onion and garlic; sauté until tender.

Add beans and water to cover; bring to a boil. Reduce heat; cover and simmer 1½ hours or until beans are tender. Add salt. Yield: 8 servings.

Fresh Green Beans: A Southern accompaniment to any meal.

BARBECUED GREEN BEANS

1½ pounds fresh green beans, snapped
2 tablespoons finely chopped onion
1 tablespoon finely chopped green pepper
¼ cup butter or margarine
¼ cup chili sauce
¼ cup vinegar
1 tablespoon prepared mustard
1 teaspoon prepared horseradish
½ teaspoon salt
½ teaspoon curry powder
⅛ teaspoon red pepper

Cook beans, covered, in a small amount of boiling salted water 1 hour or until beans are tender. Drain; reserve 1½ cups liquid.

Sauté onion and green pepper in butter in a large skillet until tender. Add chili sauce, vinegar, mustard, horseradish, salt, curry powder, red pepper, and reserved cooking liquid. Cook over medium heat 5 minutes. Add beans; simmer 10 minutes. Yield: 6 servings.

SPLIT GREEN BEANS

2 pounds fresh green beans
Pinch of baking soda
2 tablespoons butter or margarine
1½ teaspoons salt
¼ teaspoon pepper
½ cup slivered almonds

Break tips from beans; remove strings, if necessary. Wash in cold water and drain. Using a knife, cut each bean lengthwise into several slices.

Place beans, soda, and water to cover in a medium saucepan. Bring to a boil and cook 2 minutes; drain well. Return beans to saucepan; add water to cover, and bring to a boil. Reduce heat; cover and simmer 15 minutes or until tender. Drain; add butter, salt, and pepper, stirring well. Sprinkle almonds over beans to serve. Yield: 8 servings.

SWEET-AND-SOUR BEANS

1 pound fresh green beans, snapped
1 small onion, finely chopped
1 tablespoon butter or margarine
1½ teaspoons all-purpose flour
¾ cup water
¼ cup vinegar
1 tablespoon sugar
½ teaspoon salt
Pinch of pepper
2 whole cloves
1 bay leaf

Cook beans, covered, in a small amount of boiling salted water 20 minutes. Drain.

Sauté onion in butter in a medium saucepan until tender. Add flour, stirring until smooth. Cook 1 minute, stirring constantly. Combine remaining ingredients; add to onion mixture, stirring until smooth. Add beans; cover and cook over low heat 15 minutes or until beans are tender. Discard cloves and bay leaf. Yield: 4 servings.

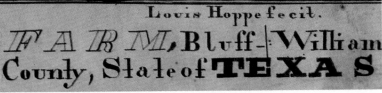

Louis Hoppe fecit.

FARM, Bluff. William County, State of TEXAS

This watercolor of Julius Meyenberg's Farm, William's Creek, c.1864, illustrates Texas farm life during the state's frontier period.

GREEN BEANS TARRAGON

2 pounds fresh green beans
2 tablespoons dried whole tarragon
¼ cup plus 2 tablespoons olive oil
2 tablespoons vinegar
4 cloves garlic, minced
2 teaspoons salt
2 teaspoons dry mustard
½ teaspoon pepper
Fresh tarragon leaves

Break tips from beans; remove strings, if necessary. Wash in cold water, and drain. Place beans with water to cover in a medium saucepan. Bring to a boil and cook 6 minutes; drain well. Cool completely.

Combine dried whole tarragon, olive oil, vinegar, garlic, salt, mustard, and pepper; mix well, and pour over beans. Cover and refrigerate overnight, tossing occasionally. Transfer to a serving dish; garnish with tarragon leaves. Yield: 8 servings.

GREEN BEANS AND NEW POTATOES

¼ pound salt pork, cut into ½-inch cubes
6 cups water
2 pounds fresh green beans, snapped
1 small onion
½ teaspoon pepper
12 new potatoes, washed and scrubbed

Place salt pork and water in a large Dutch oven; cover and cook over medium heat 1 hour. Add green beans, onion, and pepper; cover and simmer 30 minutes.

Add potatoes; cover and simmer 50 minutes or until vegetables are tender. Yield: 8 servings.

SAUTÉED GREEN BEANS

5 slices bacon
2 pounds fresh green beans, snapped
1 medium onion, chopped

Cook bacon in a large skillet until crisp; drain on paper towels. Crumble and set aside; reserve drippings in skillet.

Place crumbled bacon, beans, and onion in reserved drippings. Cook over medium heat 10 minutes, stirring occasionally. Reduce heat to low; cover and simmer 40 minutes or until tender. Yield: 8 servings.

Old-time Creole cooks had a magic touch with vegetables. The French influence is evident in a recipe calling for a bouquet of parsley, a small green onion, a laurel (bay) leaf, and a sprig of thyme tied together. The bouquet was cooked with the beans 15 minutes and withdrawn. The beans were then cooked, "dancing around in plenty of hot water," until tender.

BEETS

HOW TO PREPARE FRESH BEETS

1½ pounds small beets

To Clean and Boil: Leave root and 1 inch of stem on beets; scrub with a brush. Place beets in a medium saucepan with water to cover. Bring to a boil. Cover; reduce heat and simmer 35 minutes or until tender. Drain. Pour cold water over beets, and drain. Let cool. Trim off beet stems and roots; rub off skins. Yield: 4 servings.

Note: Care should be taken not to cut the stem too close to the beet or break off the roots. This prevents the color and sweetness from escaping from the beets during cooking.

Serving Suggestions: Beets may be seasoned with salt, pepper, and melted butter or served with Drawn Butter, Horseradish Sauce, or Oil and Lemon Sauce.

SWEET-AND-SOUR BEETS

½ pound beets, cleaned and boiled
2 cups vinegar
1 cup sugar
¾ teaspoon salt

Cut beets into ¼-inch-thick slices; set aside.

Combine vinegar, sugar, and salt in a saucepan; bring to a boil. Add beets and cover. Reduce heat; simmer 10 minutes. Remove from heat; cover and chill. Yield: 2 servings.

CREAMED BEETS

3 cups cooked, mashed beets
  (about 2 pounds)
1 medium-size banana
  pepper, minced
2 tablespoons lemon juice
1 teaspoon salt
1 (8-ounce) carton
  commercial sour cream
1 small clove garlic, halved
½ cup fine, dry breadcrumbs
2 tablespoons butter or
  margarine, melted

Combine beets, banana pepper, lemon juice, and salt. Add
sour cream. Mix well.

Rub a 1-quart casserole with
garlic; discard. Spoon beet mix-
ure into prepared dish.

Combine breadcrumbs and
butter; sprinkle over casserole.
Bake at 350° for 20 minutes.
Yield: 4 to 6 servings.

HARVARD BEETS

1 pound beets (about 2 cups),
  cleaned and boiled
3 tablespoons sugar
1 tablespoon cornstarch
½ cup water
¼ cup vinegar
1 tablespoon butter or
  margarine
½ teaspoon salt
Fresh parsley sprigs

Dice beets, and set aside.
Combine sugar and corn-
starch in a medium saucepan;
stir well. Gradually add water;
stir until smooth. Add vinegar
and butter; cook over medium
heat, stirring constantly, until
butter melts and sauce is thickened. Add beets and salt; cook
over medium heat 5 minutes or
until thoroughly heated. Garnish with parsley sprigs. Yield:
2 to 4 servings.

Harvard Beets (front)
and Creamed Beets are but
two possibilities for serving
an old-favorite root
vegetable. To hold color,
cook beets before peeling.

THE DEAD BEAT.

Late nineteenth-century
advertising trade card.

BEETS IN ORANGE SAUCE

2 pounds beets
2 cups orange juice
2 tablespoons butter or
  margarine, melted
2 teaspoons sugar
1 teaspoon salt
2 teaspoons grated orange
  rind

Wash and pare beets; cut into
¼-inch-thick slices. Place beets
in a lightly greased 12- x 8- x 2-
inch baking dish.

Combine orange juice, butter,
sugar, and salt. Pour orange
juice mixture over beets. Sprinkle grated orange rind over
beets. Cover and bake at 350°
for 1 hour or until beets are
tender. Serve immediately.
Yield: 6 to 8 servings.

BEETROOT WINE

From the English comes
this recipe for Beetroot
Wine: "Cleanse roots
thoroughly. Slice; put into
pan with 1 pint water to 1
pint roots. Boil gently until
roots sink to bottom of pan.
Strain; add 3 pounds sugar
per gallon of liquid. Boil for
half an hour. When cool, add
ground ginger and yeast.
Stir. Allow to stand 24
hours; bottle. Cork or seal
down when it has finished
working."

Secrets of Some Wiltshire Housewives, 1927

BROCCOLI

HOW TO PREPARE FRESH BROCCOLI

1 pound fresh broccoli

To Clean: Trim off large leaves and tough ends of stalks. If stalks are large, peel off outer covering with vegetable peeler. Wash thoroughly. Cut stems lengthwise from end through green head to make spears.

To Simmer: Cook broccoli, covered, in a small amount of boiling salted water 15 minutes or just until tender. Yield: 4 servings.

To Steam: Arrange broccoli spears in steaming rack with stalks to center of rack. Place over boiling water; cover and steam 20 minutes. To prepare broccoli for salads, steam 6 minutes; refresh under cold water.

Other Cooking Methods: Bake; stir-fry flowerets.

Serving Suggestions: Broccoli may be served with any of the following: Almond Butter, Cheese Sauce, Dill Sauce, Drawn Butter, French Dressing, Lemon-Butter Sauce, Mayonnaise Dressing, Tangy Butter Sauce, or any hollandaise, sour cream, or white sauce.

To Thomas Jefferson, as evidenced by the planting journals he kept, farming was an obsession. He applied his mind not only to the foods Washington knew, but also studied agriculture abroad and brought back seeds with which to experiment in his greenhouses. Around 1773, Jefferson let 2,000 acres of land to an Italian acquaintance, Philip Mazzei, for the purpose of establishing a vineyard. There is a possibility that broccoli and zucchini and other Italian seeds may have come to Monticello along with Mazzei's Tuscan laborers. Jefferson wanted to cultivate deeper than his old-style plow could turn, so he invented the mold-board plow. It won him a gold medal at a Paris exposition.

BROCCOLI BAKED WITH CHEESE SAUCE

2 pounds fresh broccoli, cleaned and cooked
2 tablespoons chopped onion
3 tablespoons butter or margarine
3 tablespoons all-purpose flour
2½ cups milk
½ cup grated Parmesan cheese
½ teaspoon salt
½ teaspoon dry mustard
¼ teaspoon pepper
¼ teaspoon paprika
⅛ teaspoon ground marjoram
¼ cup (1 ounce) shredded sharp Cheddar cheese

Place broccoli in a 12- x 8- x 2-inch baking dish. Sauté onion in butter; add flour, stirring until smooth. Cook 1 minute, stirring constantly. Gradually add milk; cook over medium heat, stirring constantly, until thickened and bubbly. Add Parmesan cheese, salt, mustard, pepper, paprika, and marjoram; stir until cheese melts. Spoon sauce over broccoli; bake at 375° for 15 minutes. Sprinkle Cheddar cheese over top; bake 5 minutes. Yield: 6 to 8 servings.

LEMON BROCCOLI

2 pounds fresh broccoli, cleaned and cooked
¼ cup butter or margarine, melted
1 tablespoon lemon juice
½ teaspoon salt
⅛ teaspoon pepper

Place broccoli spears in a serving dish. Combine remaining ingredients; stir well. Spoon over broccoli. Yield: 6 servings.

BROCCOLI SOUFFLÉ

2 tablespoons finely chopped
  onion
3 tablespoons butter or
  margarine
3 tablespoons all-purpose
  flour
1 cup milk
¾ teaspoon salt
⅛ teaspoon pepper
Dash of red pepper
4 eggs, separated
1½ cups cooked, chopped
  broccoli, well drained
1 tablespoon lemon juice
¼ teaspoon cream of tartar

Sauté chopped onion in butter in a medium saucepan until
tender; add flour, stirring until
smooth. Cook 1 minute, stirring constantly. Gradually add 1
cup milk; cook over medium
heat, stirring constantly, until
thickened and bubbly. Stir in
salt and pepper.

Beat egg yolks until thick and
lemon colored. Combine cream
sauce, beaten yolks, broccoli,
and lemon juice in a medium
mixing bowl; set aside.

Combine egg whites (at room
temperature) and cream of tartar; beat until stiff but not dry.
Gently fold egg whites into broccoli mixture. Spoon into a
lightly greased 1½-quart casserole. Place in a pan of hot water;
bake at 325° for 40 minutes.
Yield: 6 servings.

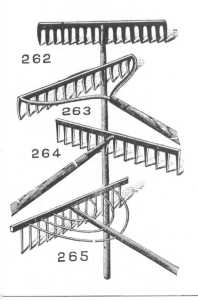

BROCCOLI PARMESAN

*Starting with fresh broccoli
and ending with cheese,
Broccoli Parmesan tastes
as good as it looks.*

2½ pounds fresh broccoli,
  cleaned and cooked
½ teaspoon salt
Dash of pepper
2 tablespoons butter or
  margarine, melted
¾ cup grated Parmesan
  cheese

Arrange broccoli in a serving
dish. Season with salt and pepper. Pour melted butter over
broccoli, and sprinkle with Parmesan cheese. Place under
broiler for 2 minutes or until
cheese is golden brown. Yield:
about 8 servings.

WINE-BUTTER BROCCOLI

2 pounds fresh broccoli,
  cleaned and steamed
2 tablespoons butter or
  margarine, melted
2 tablespoons Chablis or
  other dry white wine

Arrange broccoli spears in a
serving dish. Combine melted
butter and wine; pour over broccoli and toss lightly. Yield: 6
servings.

BRUSSELS SPROUTS

HOW TO PREPARE FRESH BRUSSELS SPROUTS

1 pound fresh brussels
   sprouts
2 tablespoons butter or
   margarine, melted
2 teaspoons lemon juice

To Clean: Trim base, and discard yellowed outer leaves. Soak brussels sprouts in heavily salted water for 10 minutes. Lift from the salt water and plunge into cool water. Rinse thoroughly. Cut a small cross in base of each brussels sprout to hasten cooking.

To Boil: Place brussels sprouts with salt water to barely cover in a saucepan. Bring to a boil. Reduce heat; simmer 20 minutes or until tender. Drain; place in serving dish. Add butter and lemon juice; toss lightly. Yield: 4 servings.

Other Cooking Methods: Steam.

Serving Suggestions: Brussels sprouts may be served with any of the following: Almond Butter, Herb Butter, Horseradish Sauce, Lemon-Butter Sauce, Mayonnaise Dressing, or any sour cream sauce.

Brussels Sprouts and Chestnuts: A combination that has become a classic. Sprouts are a relatively new form of cabbage.

BRUSSELS SPROUTS WITH CREAM

1 pound fresh brussels
  sprouts, cleaned
½ cup whipping cream
2 tablespoons butter or
  margarine
Nutmeg

Place brussels sprouts with salt water to barely cover in a small Dutch oven. Bring to a boil; reduce heat, and simmer, uncovered, 20 minutes or until tender. Drain; place in a serving dish and keep warm.

Combine cream and butter; cook over low heat until butter melts. Pour over brussels sprouts. Sprinkle with nutmeg. Yield: 4 servings.

BRUSSELS SPROUTS AND CHESTNUTS

½ cup butter or margarine,
  divided
¼ cup plus 2 tablespoons
  all-purpose flour
3 cups half-and-half
1 teaspoon salt
⅛ teaspoon pepper
1½ cups peeled and blanched
  chestnuts
½ pound fresh mushrooms,
  sliced
2 pounds fresh brussels
  sprouts, cleaned and boiled
¾ cup grated Parmesan
  cheese

Melt ¼ cup plus 2 tablespoons butter in a heavy saucepan over low heat; add flour, stirring until smooth. Cook 1 minute, stirring constantly. Gradually add half-and-half; cook over medium heat, stirring constantly, until thickened and bubbly. Stir in salt and pepper. Set aside.

Sauté chestnuts and mushrooms in 2 tablespoons butter in a large skillet for 2 minutes. Add brussels sprouts; sauté an additional 2 minutes.

Place vegetable mixture in a shallow 3-quart baking dish. Pour reserved sauce over vegetable mixture; sprinkle with cheese. Bake at 300° for 30 minutes. Yield: 12 servings.

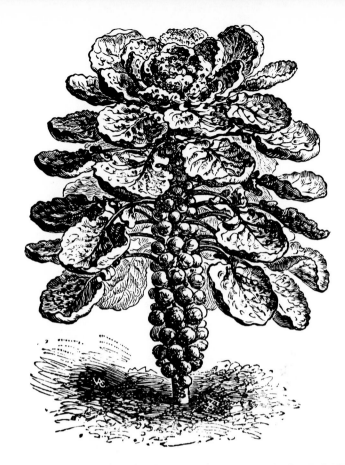

FESTIVE BRUSSELS SPROUTS

3 tablespoons butter or
  margarine, divided
1 tablespoon all-purpose flour
1 cup whipping cream
¼ teaspoon salt
¼ teaspoon pepper
1 pound fresh brussels
  sprouts, cleaned and boiled
½ cup chopped pecans

Melt 1 tablespoon butter in a heavy saucepan over low heat; add flour, stirring until smooth. Cook 1 minute, stirring constantly. Gradually add whipping cream; cook over medium heat, stirring constantly, until mixture is thickened and bubbly. Stir in salt and pepper. Add drained brussels sprouts, and toss gently. Place in a serving dish, and keep warm.

Sauté pecans in remaining 2 tablespoons butter in a small skillet about 5 minutes. Drain pecans, and sprinkle over brussels sprouts. Yield: 4 servings.

BRUSSELS SPROUTS IN BROWNED BUTTER

1 pound fresh brussels
  sprouts, cleaned
¼ cup butter
2 tablespoons apple cider
  vinegar

Place brussels sprouts with salt water to barely cover in a small Dutch oven. Bring to a boil; reduce heat, and simmer, uncovered, 20 minutes or until tender. Drain; place in a serving dish and keep warm.

Melt butter in a heavy saucepan over low heat; continue cooking 5 minutes or until butter is browned. Remove from heat and add vinegar, stirring well. Pour butter sauce over brussels sprouts; toss gently. Yield: 4 servings.

CABBAGE

HOW TO PREPARE FRESH CABBAGE

1 medium cabbage

To Clean: Discard any yellowed or withered leaves. Rinse well under cold running water. To cook whole cabbage, cut out core with a sharp knife, and discard. For other recipes, cut cabbage in half; cut out core, and discard. Cut in wedges, chop, or shred as directed in recipe.

To Boil: Cut cabbage into 6 wedges. Fill a large Dutch oven half full of water; add 1 tablespoon salt, and bring to a boil. Add cabbage wedges; let water return to a gentle boil. Cook, uncovered, 10 minutes or until cabbage is tender. Drain well. Season and serve immediately. Yield: 4 to 6 servings.

Other Cooking Methods: Bake; poêle; simmer; stir-fry.

Serving Suggestions: Cabbage may be served with butter and salt and pepper to taste or with any of the following: Basil Vinegar, Chive Blossom Vinegar, Chive Vinegar, French Dressing, Fresh Tomato Sauce, Horseradish Sauce, Hot Pepper Sauce, Lemon-Butter Sauce, Mason County Relish, or Oil and Lemon Sauce.

"Remember, from good seeds only can good vegetables be obtained," reads this 1900s ad.

BOILED CABBAGE

1 medium cabbage, cleaned
1 (½-pound) ham hock, rinsed
1 small red pepper pod
1 teaspoon salt
½ teaspoon pepper

Place all ingredients in a large Dutch oven with water to cover; bring to a boil. Reduce heat; cover and simmer 40 minutes or until cabbage is tender. Drain well, and cut into wedges to serve. Yield: 4 to 6 servings.

SCALLOPED CABBAGE

4 cups shredded cabbage (about 1 medium cabbage)
3 tablespoons butter
1½ tablespoons all-purpose flour
1½ cups milk
¾ teaspoon pepper
28 saltine crackers, crushed
2 tablespoons butter or margarine

Cook shredded cabbage, covered, in a small amount of boiling salted water for 15 minutes or until cabbage is tender; drain well. Set cooked cabbage aside, and keep warm.

Melt 3 tablespoons butter in a heavy saucepan over low heat; add flour, stirring until smooth. Cook mixture 1 minute, stirring constantly. Gradually stir in milk. Cook sauce over medium heat, stirring constantly, until thickened and bubbly. Stir in pepper.

Place one-third cracker crumbs in a lightly greased shallow 2½-quart baking dish. Spoon half of cabbage over cracker crumbs. Pour half of sauce mixture over cabbage. Repeat layers, ending with cracker crumbs. Dot cracker crumb layers with 2 tablespoons butter. Cover and bake at 350° for 30 minutes. Serve warm in baking dish. Yield: 8 servings.

SOUTHERN-COOKED CABBAGE

1 medium cabbage, cleaned
  and shredded
1 cup water
¼ pound salt pork
½ teaspoon sugar
1 teaspoon salt (optional)
⅛ teaspoon pepper (optional)

Combine shredded cabbage, water, salt pork, and sugar in a large Dutch oven. Bring to a boil. Reduce heat; cover and simmer 20 minutes or until cabbage is tender. Drain well. Season with salt and pepper, if desired. Yield: 6 servings.

CABBAGE AU GRATIN

3 tablespoons butter
3 tablespoons all-purpose
  flour
1½ cups milk
½ cup plus 2 tablespoons
  shredded process
  American cheese,
  divided
¾ teaspoon salt
½ teaspoon celery salt
½ teaspoon pepper
1 small cabbage, cleaned,
  cut into 6 wedges,
  and boiled
2 tablespoons fine dry
  breadcrumbs
1 tablespoon chopped fresh
  parsley

Melt butter in a heavy saucepan over low heat; add flour, stirring until smooth. Cook 1 minute, stirring constantly. Gradually add milk; cook over medium heat, stirring constantly, until sauce is thickened and bubbly. Add ¼ cup plus 2 tablespoons cheese, salt, celery salt, and pepper. Cook, stirring constantly, until cheese melts.

Place cabbage wedges in a shallow baking dish. Pour sauce over cabbage. Sprinkle remaining ¼ cup cheese and breadcrumbs over top. Bake at 350° for 10 minutes or until cheese melts. Sprinkle with chopped parsley and serve. Yield: 4 to 6 servings.

Bubble and Squeak, a tradition on Boxing Day in England.

BUBBLE AND SQUEAK

2 cups finely shredded
  cabbage (about 1 small
  cabbage)
1 small onion, finely chopped
3 tablespoons butter or
  margarine
Salt and pepper to taste
2 cups mashed potatoes

Cook cabbage, covered, in a small amount of boiling salted water for 15 minutes; drain well, and set aside.

Sauté onion in butter until tender. Combine cabbage and onion; add salt and pepper. Cook over low heat 2 minutes. Fold in mashed potatoes until well blended.

Spoon mixture onto a hot, lightly greased 9-inch griddle; pat mixture evenly on griddle, leaving a ½-inch margin around edge of griddle.

Cook 20 minutes or until both sides are browned, turning once. Yield: 6 servings.

TENNESSEE FRIED CABBAGE

⅓ pound salt pork, cut
   into ½-inch cubes
1 medium cabbage, cleaned
   and chopped
½ teaspoon salt

Place salt pork in a large Dutch oven; cook, uncovered, over medium heat 15 minutes or until salt pork is browned. Add chopped cabbage; cover and cook over medium heat 10 minutes. Add salt, stirring well. Cook, uncovered, an additional 10 minutes or until cabbage is tender. Serve immediately. Yield: 4 to 6 servings.

Note: Seven slices of uncooked bacon, chopped, may be substituted for salt pork to yield an equally delicious, but different, flavor.

Red Cabbage with Apples, a traditional dish brought to this country by German immigrants. Good with sauerbraten or wurst.

RED CABBAGE WITH APPLES

1 medium-size red cabbage,
   cleaned and shredded
2 tablespoons chopped onion
2 tablespoons bacon
   drippings
2 medium apples, cored and
   thinly sliced
½ teaspoon salt
½ teaspoon caraway seeds
¼ cup red wine vinegar
¼ cup firmly packed brown
   sugar

Place cabbage in cold water to soak; set aside.

Sauté onion in bacon drippings in a Dutch oven until tender.

Drain cabbage; add to sautéed onion. Cover and cook 10 minutes. Add apple slices, salt, and caraway seeds to cabbage mixture; stir lightly. Cover and cook 10 minutes or until apple slices and cabbage are tender.

Combine vinegar and sugar. Stir into cabbage mixture. Cover and simmer 5 minutes. Yield: 8 servings.

SMOTHERED RED CABBAGE

1 medium-size red cabbage,
   cleaned and shredded
2 quarts boiling water
1 small onion, finely chopped
2 tablespoons butter or
   margarine
1 tablespoon all-purpose flour
¼ cup vinegar
1 cup water
1 tablespoon firmly packed
   brown sugar
½ teaspoon salt
⅛ teaspoon pepper

Place cabbage in a large colander; pour boiling water over cabbage, and drain well. Set aside.

Sauté onion in butter in a Dutch oven until tender. Add cabbage; cover and cook over low heat 10 minutes.

Dissolve flour in vinegar, stirring with a wire whisk until smooth. Add flour mixture, 1 cup water, sugar, salt, and pepper to cabbage. Cover and cook over low heat 50 minutes or until cabbage is tender. Yield: 6 to 8 servings.

Shredded on a "mandoline" or chopped with special cutters, sauerkraut had to be salted and packed down.

GERMAN SAUERKRAUT

1 small onion, chopped
1 medium apple, peeled, cored, and chopped
2 tablespoons bacon drippings
1 (32-ounce) jar sauerkraut
1 tablespoon caraway seeds
1 teaspoon salt
1½ cups water
1 small baking potato, peeled and grated

Sauté onion and apple in hot bacon drippings in a Dutch oven until tender. Add sauerkraut, caraway seeds, salt, and water. Bring to a boil. Reduce heat; cover and simmer 1 hour and 15 minutes. Stir in potato; simmer 30 minutes. Cool. Cover and refrigerate overnight. Yield: 6 to 8 servings.

Serving Suggestions: German Sauerkraut may be served cold or hot with corned beef or frankfurters.

WINE SAUERKRAUT

2 (1-pound) heads cabbage, cleaned, shredded, and boiled
1 medium onion, chopped
½ cup butter or margarine
¼ cup sugar
2 cups dry white wine
½ teaspoon salt
⅛ teaspoon pepper

Sauté onion in butter until tender. Add sugar; cook until sugar dissolves; stir constantly.

Combine sautéed onion mixture, cabbage, wine, salt, and pepper in a Dutch oven. Cover and cook over low heat 1 hour. Yield: 8 servings.

Marion Harland, witty culinary savant, began her sauerkraut by lining a container with cabbage leaves. Then came layers of 3 inches of chopped or shredded cabbage strewn with 4 tablespoons salt. Every fifth layer was compacted with a wooden beetle, and another layer of leaves added. At last, the vessel full, she weighted it down heavily and set it away for 3 weeks, making one of her typical notations: "This. . .to nostrils unaccustomed to it, is a malodorous compound."

CARROTS

HOW TO PREPARE FRESH CARROTS

1 pound carrots

To Clean: Wash carrots; peel with vegetable peeler or scrape, if preferred. Cut stem end evenly. Baby carrots may be cooked whole; larger carrots should be cut into ⅛- to ¼-inch-thick slices before cooking. For use in soups and stews, simply scrub carrots well and use without peeling.

To Boil: Cook cleaned carrots in a small amount of boiling salted water 10 minutes or until carrots are tender; drain well. Yield: 4 servings.

To Steam: Arrange carrots in steaming rack; place over boiling water. Cover and steam 12 minutes or until crisp-tender.

Other Cooking Methods: Parboil or steam, and then deep-fry; simmer; stir-fry/steam; poêle.

Serving Suggestions: Carrots may be served with melted butter and seasonings to taste or with any of the following: Almond Butter, Cream Mint Spread, Dill Sauce, Horseradish Sauce, Lemon-Butter Sauce, Oil and Lemon sauce; any herb butter or spread; or any hollandaise or white sauce.

Carrot Balls (bottom) and Shaker Lemon-Glazed Carrots. The Trustees House dining room, Shakertown at Pleasant Hill, Kentucky, serves fresh vegetables from its own garden.

CANDIED CARROTS IN ORANGE RINGS

1 orange
12 baby carrots, cleaned
1½ cups boiling water
2 tablespoons butter or
  margarine
½ cup sugar
Dash of salt

Slice orange into four ½-inch-thick slices.

Make a small slit in the center of each orange slice, and insert 3 carrots through each.

Place carrot rings in a small saucepan; add water. Cover and cook until carrots are crisp-tender. Drain, reserving ¼ cup cooking liquid.

Melt butter in a small saucepan; stir in sugar, salt, and reserved liquid. Cook over low heat until sugar dissolves. Spoon glaze over carrots and orange slices to serve. Yield: 4 servings.

CARROT BALLS

2 cups sliced carrots, cooked
  and mashed
1½ cups soft breadcrumbs
1 cup (4 ounces) shredded
  sharp Cheddar cheese
½ teaspoon salt
¼ teaspoon pepper
Dash of hot sauce
1 egg white
1¼ cups coarsely crushed
  cornflakes

Combine carrots, breadcrumbs, cheese, salt, pepper, and hot sauce; toss lightly. Beat egg white (at room temperature) until stiff peaks form; fold into carrot mixture. (Mixture may be chilled at this stage.)

Shape mixture into 2-inch balls; roll in cornflakes. Place balls on a lightly greased baking sheet. Bake at 375° for 30 minutes or until golden brown. Yield: 1 dozen.

Mr. Carrot escorts pretty Miss Turnip in this advertisement for Martin & Roach's Restaurant, 1885.

SHAKER LEMON-GLAZED CARROTS

1½ pounds baby carrots,
  cleaned and cooked
⅓ cup sugar
2 tablespoons firmly packed
  brown sugar
2 tablespoons butter or
  margarine
2 teaspoons lemon juice

Place whole, cooked carrots in a 1-quart baking dish.

Combine brown sugar, butter, and lemon juice in a small saucepan; bring to a boil. Reduce heat to low, and simmer 10 minutes or until mixture is thickened. Pour over carrots, and bake at 450° for 15 minutes. Yield: 4 servings.

Mothers were saying "Carrots are good for you" long before they knew the connection between Vitamin A and good vision. For centuries, English sailors ate limes to keep from getting scurvy, not knowing it was Vitamin C keeping them healthy. Casimir Funk, a biochemist, discovered vitamins around 1900, naming them for the Latin *vita* — meaning life.

CARROT FRITTERS

1½ cups cleaned, shredded
  baby carrots (about 1 dozen)
3 cups soft breadcrumbs
½ cup milk
2 eggs, beaten
3 tablespoons minced onion
¾ teaspoon baking powder
¼ teaspoon salt
⅛ teaspoon pepper
Vegetable oil

Combine first 8 ingredients; mix well. Heat 2 inches of oil in a heavy skillet over medium heat. Drop mixture by table-spoonfuls into hot oil (375°). Fry until golden brown, turning once; drain. Serve hot. Yield: about 1½ dozen.

Serving Suggestion: Carrot Fritters may be served as an appetizer with Horseradish Sauce.

FRIED CARROTS

3 large carrots, cleaned and
  sliced into thin strips
1 teaspoon salt
1 egg, beaten
1 cup buttery cracker
  crumbs
Vegetable oil

Place carrots and salt in a small saucepan; add water to cover. Bring to a boil; reduce heat and cook 10 minutes or until tender. Drain. Dip carrot strips, a few at a time, into egg; dredge in cracker crumbs.

Fry strips in hot oil (375°) until golden brown; drain on paper towels. Serve hot. Yield: about 2 dozen.

Serving Suggestion: Fried Carrots may be served with Dill Sauce.

SWEET-AND-SOUR CARROTS

1 pound carrots, cleaned and
  cut into 1-inch slices
½ cup vinegar
½ cup beef broth
½ cup sugar
1 tablespoon all-purpose flour

Cook carrots in a small amount of boiling salted water 10 minutes or until crisp-tender; drain and set aside.

Combine vinegar and broth in a saucepan; bring to a boil. Reduce heat; simmer 2 minutes.

Combine sugar and flour; stir well, and sprinkle in a 10-inch cast-iron skillet. Place over medium heat, stirring constantly with a wooden spoon until sugar melts and becomes a light golden brown. Gradually add vinegar-broth mixture, stirring to make a smooth syrup. Add carrots; cook over medium heat 15 minutes or until carrots are tender. Yield: 2 to 4 servings.

CARROT RING

3 eggs
2¼ cups cooked, mashed
  carrots (about 2 pounds)
1 cup soft breadcrumbs
1 cup whipping cream
¾ cup (3 ounces) shredded
  sharp Cheddar cheese
½ cup chopped pecans
2 tablespoons butter or
  margarine, melted
1 tablespoon minced onion
¾ teaspoon salt
¼ teaspoon ground nutmeg
¼ teaspoon white pepper
⅛ teaspoon red pepper

Beat eggs in a large mixing bowl until thick and lemon colored; add remaining ingredients, mixing well.

Spoon into a well-greased 4-cup ovenproof ring mold. Bake at 350° for 1 hour. Remove from oven; cool on wire rack 40 minutes. Yield: 8 to 10 servings.

Serving Suggestion: Carrot Ring may be filled with Celery with Mushrooms or Southern-Cooked Green Peas.

Varieties of carrots from an 1888 book on gardening.

CAULIFLOWER

HOW TO PREPARE FRESH CAULIFLOWER

1 medium head cauliflower

To Clean: Wash cauliflower; remove slight discolorations with a vegetable peeler. Trim stalk, removing core; remove outer leaves. Leave whole or break into flowerets, discarding inner core. If served whole, a few leaves left at base of cauliflower are attractive.

To Boil: Place cauliflower, head side down, in boiling salted water. Cover and cook over medium heat 15 minutes or until crisp-tender. Drain well. Yield: 6 servings.

Note: For a whiter cauliflower, simmer in whole or skim milk rather than water.

To Steam: Arrange flowerets on steaming rack. Place over boiling water; cover and steam 10 minutes or until crisp-tender. Yield: 6 servings.

Other Cooking Methods: Parboil cauliflower head, and then bake; deep-fry cauliflower flowerets.

Serving Suggestions: Cauliflower may be served with Cheese Sauce, Hollandaise Sauce Supreme, Mock Hollandaise Sauce, or any sour cream sauce.

Cauliflower au Gratin — irresistible!

CAULIFLOWER AU GRATIN

1 small onion, chopped
1 tablespoon butter or margarine
1 cup milk
1½ cups (6 ounces) shredded American cheese, divided
1 egg yolk, beaten
¼ teaspoon salt
⅛ teaspoon white pepper
⅛ teaspoon paprika
1 medium head cauliflower, cleaned and cooked
½ cup soft breadcrumbs

Sauté onion in butter in a saucepan until tender. Add milk; cook over low heat 5 minutes. Add 1 cup cheese; cook, stirring constantly, until cheese melts. Cool.

Stir in egg yolk, salt, pepper, and paprika. Spoon ¼ cup of sauce into a 2-quart baking dish. Place cauliflower in sauce. Spoon remaining sauce over cauliflower. Top with remaining cheese and breadcrumbs.

Bake at 350° for 15 minutes or until lightly browned. Yield: 6 servings.

Wagonload of cauliflower and other vegetables bound for San Antonio, c.1908.

CAULIFLOWER MAÎTRE D'HOTEL

¼ cup butter or margarine, melted
1 tablespoon chopped fresh parsley
1 tablespoon lemon juice
1 teaspoon paprika
½ teaspoon salt
1 medium head cauliflower, cleaned and cooked
1 hard-cooked egg, finely chopped (optional)

Combine butter, parsley, lemon juice, paprika, and salt; mix well.

Place cauliflower in a serving dish. Pour sauce over cauliflower. Sprinkle with chopped egg, if desired. Yield: 6 servings.

CAULIFLOWER DUCHESSE

1 medium head cauliflower
½ cup butter or margarine
3 tablespoons vinegar
2 tablespoons chopped pimiento, drained
2 tablespoons chopped green pepper
1 tablespoon sugar
¼ teaspoon salt

Wash cauliflower, and break into flowerets. Cook, covered, in a small amount of boiling salted water 10 minutes or until crisp-tender. Drain and place in a serving dish. Set aside.

Combine butter, vinegar, chopped pimiento, chopped green pepper, sugar, and salt in a small saucepan. Bring mixture to a boil. Remove from heat, and pour over flowerets. Yield: 6 servings.

CREOLE CAULIFLOWER

1 small head cauliflower
1 medium onion, chopped
1 small green pepper, chopped
¼ cup butter or margarine
3 tablespoons all-purpose flour
1 (14½-ounce) can whole tomatoes, chopped
½ teaspoon salt
¼ teaspoon pepper
½ cup (2 ounces) shredded Cheddar cheese

Wash cauliflower and break into flowerets. Cook, covered, in a small amount of boiling salted water 10 minutes or until crisp-tender; drain. Set aside.

Sauté onion and green pepper in butter in a large saucepan until tender; add flour, stirring well. Cook 1 minute, stirring constantly. Stir in cauliflower, tomatoes, salt, and pepper, mixing well. Cook over medium heat 3 minutes or until thoroughly heated.

Spoon mixture into a 1½-quart casserole; top with cheese. Bake at 350° for 5 minutes or until cheese melts. Yield: 6 servings.

FRIED CAULIFLOWER

1 medium head cauliflower
1½ cups fine, dry breadcrumbs
1 teaspoon salt
2 eggs, beaten
Vegetable oil

Wash cauliflower, and break into flowerets. Cook, covered, in a small amount of boiling salted water 10 minutes or until crisp-tender; drain.

Combine breadcrumbs and salt. Dip cauliflower in egg. Coat with breadcrumbs. Deep-fry in hot oil (375°) until golden brown. Drain well on paper towels. Serve immediately. Yield: about 2½ dozen.

Serving Suggestions: Fried Cauliflower may be served with Mustard Dip Sauce or Horseradish Sauce.

BAKED CAULIFLOWER

1 medium head cauliflower, cleaned and cooked
⅓ cup fine, dry breadcrumbs
¼ cup butter or margarine, melted

Place cauliflower in a 3-quart casserole; sprinkle with breadcrumbs. Pour melted butter over breadcrumbs and bake, uncovered, at 350° for 15 minutes. Yield: 6 servings.

"Cauliflower should be soaked 20 minutes head down. Then it is tied up in a cloth and boiled head down, like a martyr! Take it out, untie it, set it in a baking dish, and sprinkle with grated Parmesan cheese, then buttered breadcrumbs. Bake it, and serve it with sauce."

200 Years of New Orleans Cooking, 1931

Early 1900s ad for the finest in cauliflower seeds.

D.M. FERRY & CO'S
EARLY SNOWBALL
CAULIFLOWER

THE BEST VARIETY IN CULTIVATION.
EXTRA EARLY. SURE TO HEAD.
ONLY TEN CENTS PER PACKET.

CELERY

HOW TO PREPARE FRESH CELERY

1 bunch celery
1 teaspoon salt
1 tablespoon butter
1 tablespoon lemon
   juice

To Clean: Cut off base of celery and separate the stalks. Wash under cold water, using a stiff brush. To remove heavier strings from outer stalks, make a cut in the narrow end of the stalk; grasp the strings between the knife edge and thumb, and pull down toward base of celery. Discard strings. Celery may be sliced diagonally or cut in lengths horizontally and sliced in sticks. Reserve celery leaves for use in salads, as a garnish, or to add flavor to cooked celery dishes.

To Braise: Place celery, cut as desired, in a medium saucepan. Add salt, butter, lemon juice, and water to cover; bring to a boil. Cover; reduce heat and simmer 20 minutes or until celery is tender. Drain well. Yield: 2 to 4 servings.

Other Cooking Methods: Bake; deep-fry after parboiling; steam; stir-fry.

Serving Suggestions: Braised celery may be served with any of the following: Almond Butter, Dill Sauce, Drawn Butter, French Dressing, Lemon-Butter Sauce, any hollandaise, sour cream, or white sauce.

CELERY AND PECAN CASSEROLE

3 large bunches celery,
   cleaned and cut into ½-inch
   slices (about 3 cups)
1 tablespoon sugar
1 cup pecan halves
¼ cup butter or margarine
3 tablespoons all-purpose
   flour
1 cup half-and-half
1 egg, beaten
1 teaspoon salt
¼ to ½ teaspoon red pepper
½ cup buttery cracker
   crumbs

Combine celery, sugar, and water to cover in a medium saucepan. Bring to a boil. Reduce heat; cover and simmer 20 minutes or until celery is tender. Drain well. Place celery and pecans in a lightly greased 1½-quart casserole. Set aside.

Melt butter in a heavy saucepan over low heat; gradually blend in flour, and cook 1 minute, stirring constantly. Gradually add half-and-half, stirring constantly.

Gradually stir about one-fourth of hot flour mixture into egg; add to remaining mixture in saucepan, stirring well. Add salt and pepper; cook 1 minute, stirring constantly. Pour sauce over celery mixture.

Sprinkle cracker crumbs over top of casserole. Bake, uncovered, at 325° for 30 minutes. Yield: 6 servings.

CELERY WITH MUSHROOMS

2 cups sliced celery
¼ cup chopped fresh celery
   leaves
¼ pound fresh mushrooms,
   sliced
1 tablespoon butter or
   margarine
1 tablespoon all-purpose flour
½ cup half-and-half
¼ teaspoon salt
⅛ teaspoon pepper
⅛ teaspoon paprika

Combine celery, celery leaves, mushrooms, and water to cover in a medium saucepan. Bring to a boil. Reduce heat; cover and simmer 20 minutes or until vegetables are tender. Drain well, and set aside.

Melt butter in a heavy saucepan over low heat; add flour, stirring until smooth. Cook 1 minute, stirring constantly. Gradually add half-and-half; cook over medium heat, stirring constantly, until thickened and bubbly. Stir in salt, pepper, and paprika. Stir celery mixture into sauce. Yield: 4 servings.

1894 Manual of Everything for the Garden advertised this "Pink Plume" variety of celery, as the "ne plus ultra," and claimed it to be "the most beautiful celery that ever graced a table."

ENDERSON'S PINK PLUME CELERY.

PETER HENDERSON & Co.

1894.

FRENCH FRIED CELERY

6 stalks celery, cleaned and
  cut into 3- to 4-inch pieces
2 eggs, beaten
½ teaspoon salt
¼ teaspoon pepper
1 cup cracker crumbs
Vegetable oil

Cook celery, covered, in boiling salted water 15 minutes or
just until tender; drain.

Combine eggs, salt, and pepper. Dip celery pieces in egg
mixture; roll in cracker crumbs.
Deep-fry in hot oil (375°) until
golden brown. Drain on paper
towels, and serve immediately.
Yield: 4 appetizer servings.

Serving Suggestion: French
Fried Celery may be served with
Mustard Dip Sauce.

FLORIDA SIMMERED CELERY

1 chicken-flavored bouillon
  cube
1 cup boiling water
1 tablespoon onion, finely
  chopped
1 tablespoon chopped fresh
  parsley
1 tablespoon finely chopped
  fresh celery leaves
2 tablespoons butter or
  margarine
2 large bunches celery,
  cleaned and cut into ½-inch
  slices (about 3 cups)
⅛ teaspoon marjoram
⅛ teaspoon salt
Dash of pepper
2 teaspoons cornstarch

Dissolve bouillon cube in boiling water; set aside. Sauté
onion, parsley, and celery leaves
in butter in a heavy skillet until
onion is tender. Add ⅓ cup
bouillon, celery, marjoram, salt,
and pepper, mixing well.

Bring to a boil. Reduce heat;
cover and simmer 20 minutes.

Dissolve cornstarch in remaining ⅔ cup bouillon; add to
celery mixture, stirring well.
Bring to a boil; cook, stirring
constantly, until thickened and
bubbly. Yield: 4 servings.

CELERY COLLE

1 egg
¼ cup vegetable oil
1 teaspoon sugar
1 teaspoon salt
1 teaspoon dry mustard
⅛ teaspoon pepper
1 cup vegetable oil, divided
3 tablespoons vinegar
1 teaspoon prepared mustard
1 hard-cooked egg, chopped
4 large bunches celery,
  cleaned and cut into ½-inch
  slices (about 6 cups)

Combine first 6 ingredients in
container of electric blender;
process 3 seconds on high.

Turn blender to low speed;
uncover and add ½ cup oil in a
slow, steady stream. Add vinegar and remaining oil; blend
until thickened. Add mustard
and chopped egg; cover and
blend on high speed until
smooth. Chill thoroughly. Pour
sauce over celery, and stir well.
Yield: 8 servings.

*Florida Simmered Celery
(top) and the ultimate
in crispness, French
Fried Celery — unusual
side dishes.*

Today's crudité tray
may include celery
"brushes": Cut stalks
into 2-inch lengths. Make
many knife cuts ¾ inch toward center from each end.
Place in ice water to crisp
and curl.

"A Secret: To Make Celery
Crisp As A Cracker. To crisp
old celery like magic: Cut celery into 4-inch pieces. Place
in water to cover in a bowl.

Cut a medium potato into
about six pieces. Add to bowl
containing celery. Chill."
(From *Famous Old New Or-
leans Recipes.*)

CORN

HOW TO PREPARE FRESH CORN

6 ears fresh corn
1 teaspoon sugar

To Clean: Corn should be as fresh as possible since it loses its sweetness in a few hours after being picked from the stalk. To retain freshness leave in husks until just before servings. Remove husks by pulling down from top of ear. Cut or break stem off at base of ear. Remove silks using a stiff, dry vegetable brush. Trim tip, and remove blemishes with a knife, if necessary.

To Cut Kernels: Hold an ear of corn securely in one hand, resting the base of the ear in a large bowl. Using a sharp knife, cut down the length of the ear to the base; cut through the kernels, being careful not to cut into the tough cob. Rotate ear, and repeat procedure until all kernels are removed from ear. Scrape cob to remove any remaining pulp.

To Scrape Kernels: Hold the ear of corn securely in one hand. Using the tip of a sharp knife, slice through the center of a row of kernels from the base to the tip. Repeat procedure until all kernels are sliced. Holding the ear securely in one hand, rest base of ear in a large bowl. Using the back of the knife, scrape down the ear to remove the flesh and milk; rotate ear and continue scraping procedure until all flesh and milk are removed from the ear.

To Steam Corn On The Cob: Arrange corn on steaming rack. Place rack in steamer over 1 inch of water. Bring to a boil. Cover and steam for 10 minutes or until corn is crisp-tender.

To Boil Corn On The Cob: Combine sugar and enough water to half fill a large saucepan. Bring water to a boil; add corn. Return to a boil; cover, and cook 10 minutes or until corn is tender. Drain well. Yield: 6 servings.

Other Cooking Methods: Bake corn on the cob; fry, deep-fry, or stew after cutting or scraping kernels from the cob.

Serving Suggestions: Corn on the cob may be served with melted butter and salt to taste or any of the following: Drawn Butter, Lemon-Butter Sauce, or any herb butter or spread.

Two hundred and nine bushels of corn were harvested from one Virginia acre, c.1910.

Valentine Museum, Richmond, Virginia

43

"Husky" lady graces late nineteenth-century advertising card.

TENNESSEE STEWED CORN

12 ears fresh corn, cleaned
   and kernels scraped from
   cob
¼ cup water
1 cup milk
2 tablespoons butter or
   margarine
1 teaspoon salt
½ teaspoon pepper

Combine corn and water in a
large saucepan. Bring to a boil.
Reduce heat and simmer, uncovered, 20 minutes.

Add remaining ingredients.
Simmer 20 minutes; stir frequently. Yield: 6 to 8 servings.

MAQUE CHOU

2 tablespoons shortening
1 medium onion, coarsely
   chopped
½ cup chopped green
   pepper
12 ears fresh corn, cleaned
   and kernels cut
   from cob
1 cup chopped tomatoes
¼ cup milk
1¼ teaspoons salt
½ teaspoon sugar
⅛ teaspoon pepper
Dash of red pepper
1 tablespoon butter or
   margarine

Melt shortening in a large
Dutch oven. Add onion and
green pepper; sauté until
tender. Add corn, tomatoes,
milk, salt, sugar, and pepper.
Cook, uncovered, over medium
heat 30 minutes, stirring frequently. Stir in butter before
serving. Yield: 6 to 8 servings.

SOUTHERN FRIED CORN

¼ cup bacon drippings
10 ears fresh corn,
   cleaned and kernels cut
   from cob
¼ cup milk
1 teaspoon salt
½ teaspoon pepper

Heat bacon drippings in a
large skillet over medium heat.
Add corn kernels, and cook 5
minutes. Stir in ¼ cup milk,
salt, and pepper. Cook, uncovered, over medium heat 30 minutes, stirring frequently. Yield:
4 to 6 servings.

SAUTÉED WHITE CORN

¼ cup butter or margarine
12 ears fresh white corn,
   cleaned and kernels cut
   from cob
¼ cup milk
1 teaspoon salt
¼ teaspoon pepper

Melt butter in a large skillet
over medium heat. Add remaining ingredients. Cover; cook
over low heat 20 minutes, stirring occasionally. Uncover; cook
an additional 20 minutes, stirring frequently. Yield: 6 to 8
servings.

FRESH CORN CASSEROLE

2 large onions, chopped
1 tablespoon shortening
2 cups fresh corn kernels
  (about 4 ears fresh corn)
1 (14½-ounce) can whole
  tomatoes, undrained and
  chopped
2 medium-size green peppers,
  chopped
1 cup chopped celery
1 teaspoon salt
½ teaspoon pepper
3 cups soft breadcrumbs,
  divided
½ cup (2 ounces) shredded
  Cheddar cheese

Sauté onion in shortening in a Dutch oven until tender. Add corn, tomatoes, green pepper, celery, salt, and pepper. Cook over medium heat 10 minutes, stirring frequently to prevent vegetables from sticking.

Soak 2 cups soft breadcrumbs in a small amount of water. Drain well. Add to corn mixture; stir well. Spoon mixture into a well-greased 1½-quart casserole. Sprinkle with remaining 1 cup soft breadcrumbs. Bake at 350° for 20 minutes. Remove from oven, and sprinkle with cheese. Return to oven just until cheese melts. Yield: 6 servings.

Marion Harland was constantly demonstrating the practicality that gave *Common Sense in the Household* its name. Note her instructions for Roasted Green Corn: "Turn back the husks upon the stalk, pick off the silk, recover with the husks closely as possible, and roast in the hot ashes of a wood-fire. Eat with butter, salt, and pepper, out of doors, in the forest, or on the beach."

Husking sweet corn closes the generation gap. Photo by Dorothea Lange, 1941.

CORN PANCAKES

2 cups fresh corn kernels
  (about 4 ears fresh corn)
2 eggs, beaten
2 tablespoons butter or
  margarine, melted
½ teaspoon salt
2 tablespoons milk
½ cup plus 2 tablespoons
  all-purpose flour

Combine corn and eggs; add butter and salt. Mix well. Stir in milk and flour, blending well.

For each pancake, pour ¼ cup batter onto a hot, lightly greased griddle or skillet. Turn pancakes when tops are covered with bubbles and edges are browned. Yield: 8 pancakes.

CORN FRITTERS

1 tablespoon butter or
  margarine
2 tablespoons all-purpose
  flour
1 cup milk
2 eggs, beaten
¼ cup (1 ounce) shredded
  Cheddar cheese
1 teaspoon sugar
1 teaspoon salt
1 teaspoon pepper
2 cups fresh corn kernels
  (about 4 ears fresh corn)
Vegetable oil
2 eggs, beaten
1½ cups cracker crumbs

Melt butter in a heavy saucepan over low heat; add flour, stirring until smooth. Cook 1 minute, stirring constantly.

Combine milk and eggs; gradually add to flour mixture, and cook over medium heat, stirring constantly, until thickened and bubbly. Add cheese, sugar, salt, pepper, and corn; stir until cheese melts. Pour corn mixture into a greased 8-inch square pan, and freeze until firm.

Heat 1 inch of oil to 375°. Cut frozen corn mixture into 4-inch strips; dip each strip in beaten eggs and roll in cracker crumbs. Fry frozen strips in hot oil until golden brown on all sides; drain on paper towels. Yield: about 1 dozen.

Fresh Corn Oysters (rear) and Corn Pancakes.

PLANTATION CORN PUDDING

2 cups fresh corn kernels
  (about 4 ears fresh corn)
¼ cup all-purpose flour
1 tablespoon sugar
1¼ teaspoons salt
⅛ teaspoon pepper
2 cups whipping cream
4 eggs, beaten
1 tablespoon butter or
  margarine, melted

Combine corn, flour, sugar, salt, and pepper; stir well. Combine remaining ingredients, mixing well; stir into the corn mixture.

Pour into a lightly greased 1½-quart casserole. Place casserole in a pan of warm water. Bake at 350° for 1 hour and 10 minutes or until a knife inserted in center comes out clean. Yield: 6 to 8 servings.

FRESH CORN OYSTERS

1 cup all-purpose flour
1 teaspoon baking powder
1 teaspoon salt
1 egg, beaten
3 cups fresh corn kernels
  (about 6 ears fresh corn)
2 tablespoons whipping
  cream
1 tablespoon butter or
  margarine, melted
Vegetable oil

Combine flour, baking powder, and salt in a medium mixing bowl; mix well. Combine egg, corn, whipping cream, and butter; mix well, and stir into dry ingredients.

Drop mixture by tablespoonfuls into hot oil (375°); cook until golden brown, turning once. Drain on paper towels; serve hot. Yield: about 2 dozen.

HOMINY

BACON HOMINY

6 slices bacon
1 medium onion, chopped
1 (29-ounce) can hominy,
   drained
1 (10¾-ounce) can tomato
   soup, undiluted
½ cup water
1 teaspoon sugar
½ teaspoon salt
Dash of pepper

Cook bacon in a large skillet until crisp. Remove bacon, reserving drippings in skillet; crumble bacon, and set aside.

Sauté onion in bacon drippings until tender. Add bacon, hominy, soup, water, sugar, salt, and pepper. Simmer, uncovered, for 30 minutes. Yield: 4 to 6 servings.

CHILI HOMINY

1 medium onion, chopped
2 tablespoons shortening,
   melted
2 cups yellow hominy,
   drained
1 clove garlic, minced
2 teaspoons chili powder
1 teaspoon salt
2 cups (8 ounces) shredded
   Cheddar cheese

Sauté onion in shortening in a heavy skillet until tender. Add hominy and water to cover (about 1 cup). Cook, uncovered, over medium heat 15 minutes, stirring frequently. Add garlic, chili powder, and salt; stir well. Cook an additional 5 minutes. Add cheese; cook over low heat until cheese melts, stirring well. Yield: 4 to 6 servings.

SPANISH HOMINY

1 medium onion, chopped
2 tablespoons chopped green
   pepper
¼ cup plus 2 tablespoons
   bacon drippings
1 (14½-ounce) can whole
   tomatoes, drained and
   chopped
1 (14½-ounce) can hominy,
   drained
½ teaspoon salt
½ teaspoon chili powder
¼ teaspoon pepper

Sauté onion and green pepper in bacon drippings in a large skillet until tender. Add tomatoes; cook over medium heat 15 minutes. Add remaining ingredients; cook an additional 15 minutes, stirring occasionally. Yield: 4 servings.

Bacon Hominy: Easy, now that hominy comes in cans.

H ominy is one of the American South's indigenous foods, already a staple when the settlers landed. The Europeans learned from the Indians how to make hominy from corn too dry for human teeth to chew. They built ash pits in their fireplaces to make lye needed to soak the outer covering from the kernels. After soaking in lye water, the corn was well washed and put by for winter. It was eaten boiled and seasoned with salt, pepper, and butter or other fat.

Later farms had samp mills or hominy blocks to grind the whole hominy into smaller particles known as grits. Hominy was the "potatoes of the South," and grits have been called Southern ice cream, an appellation now taken as a compliment by the natives.

CUCUMBERS

HOW TO PREPARE FRESH CUCUMBERS

3 medium-size fresh
  cucumbers
¼ cup butter or margarine

To Clean: Fresh garden cucumbers may be washed for cooking or for salads without peeling. Large, waxed, out-of-season cucumbers should be peeled since the skin is unpleasant to eat, and seeds should be scraped out with a spoon. Cucumbers may be cut into halves, or quarters, or thinly sliced, as directed in recipe.

To Sauté: Cut cucumbers into ¼-inch-thick slices. Melt butter in a large skillet over medium-high heat. Add cucumbers and sauté, stirring constantly, until just tender. Season with salt, pepper, and additional butter, if desired. Serve immediately. Yield: 4 servings.

Other Cooking Methods: Parboil, and then stuff and bake; batter and deep-fry; steam.

Serving Suggestions: Sautéed cucumbers may be served with any hollandaise, sour cream, or white sauce. Fresh cucumbers may be thinly sliced and served raw with any of the following: Basil Vinegar, Chive Vinegar, Cream Mint Spread, Dill Sauce, French Dressing, Homemade Mayonnaise, or Oil and Lemon Sauce.

Another vegetable personified: Jaunty Cucumberman for Rice's Seeds, 1887.

STUFFED CUCUMBERS

3 medium cucumbers
4 slices bacon
1 small onion, chopped
1 medium tomato, peeled and
  chopped
½ cup soft breadcrumbs
½ teaspoon salt
¼ teaspoon pepper
¼ cup water

Wash cucumbers, and cut in half lengthwise. Remove pulp, leaving a ¼-inch shell. Chop pulp, and set aside.

Cook bacon in a large skillet until crisp; drain well, reserving 2 tablespoons bacon drippings in skillet. Crumble bacon, and set aside.

Sauté onion and reserved cucumber pulp in bacon drippings until tender. Add tomato, breadcrumbs, salt, and pepper.

Place cucumber shells in a 13- x 9- x 2-inch baking dish. Spoon mixture into shells; top with bacon. Pour water around cucumbers. Bake at 350° for 45 minutes or until cucumbers are tender. Yield: 6 servings.

OKLAHOMA-STYLE FRIED CUCUMBERS

2 medium cucumbers, peeled
  and cut into ¼-inch slices
2 eggs, beaten
1½ cups fine, dry
  breadcrumbs
Vegetable oil

Dip cucumber slices in egg; dredge in breadcrumbs. Fry cucumber slices in hot oil (375°) in a skillet until browned, turning once. Drain well on paper towels. Yield: about 3 dozen.

Serving Suggestions: Oklahoma-Style Fried Cucumbers may be served with any of the following: Dill Sauce, Horseradish Sauce, Mustard Dip Sauce, or any sour cream sauce.

Stuffed Cucumbers (rear) and Oklahoma-Style Fried Cucumbers.

The cucumber's history goes back over 3,000 years to India, where its cooling power made it welcome as one of the small side dishes that complement the flavor of curries. Our English forebears knew them as cowcumbers, and they brought to the new world both the variant spelling and their tradition of serving cucumber sandwiches at teatime—and Southerners still serve them: Slice cucumber thinly, sprinkle lightly with salt, and let stand 15 minutes, a technique the French call *degorger*. Towel-dry; sandwich between buttered bread slices.

FLORIDA SAUTÉED CUCUMBERS

2 tablespoons butter or margarine
2 tablespoons finely chopped onion
3 medium cucumbers, peeled and thinly sliced
½ teaspoon salt
Dash of pepper
Pinch of dried whole dillweed
¼ cup commercial sour cream
1 teaspoon chopped fresh parsley

Combine butter, onion, cucumber, salt, pepper, and dillweed in a heavy skillet. Cook over medium heat 10 minutes or until cucumber is crisp-tender. Remove from heat; add sour cream and parsley, tossing well. Cover and refrigerate at least 1 hour. Yield: 4 servings.

Serving Suggestion: Florida Sautéed Cucumbers may be served as an accompaniment to fish, veal, or chicken dishes.

BRAISED CUCUMBERS

¼ cup butter or margarine
1 tablespoon sugar
½ teaspoon salt
2 large cucumbers, peeled and cut into 1-inch slices
1 medium onion, chopped
2 medium tomatoes, peeled and cut into eighths
¼ cup water
1 teaspoon lemon juice
1 teaspoon dried whole dillweed
½ cup commercial sour cream

Melt butter in a heavy saucepan over medium heat. Add sugar and salt; cook until lightly browned. Add cucumber and onion; cook, stirring constantly, until onion is tender. Add tomatoes, water, lemon juice, and dillweed. Cook an additional 12 minutes. Remove from heat; stir in sour cream. Serve immediately. Yield: 4 servings.

Cucumber harvest at West Point, Virginia, c.1930. Everyone pitched in to help bag them for market.

EGGPLANT

HOW TO PREPARE FRESH EGGPLANT

1 large eggplant, peeled and
   cut into 1-inch cubes
1 teaspoon vinegar
Salt and pepper to taste

To Clean: Eggplant may be peeled and cut into ½-inch slices or cubed as directed in recipe. Sprinkle lightly with salt; let stand 15 minutes. Rinse and drain; wipe dry before proceeding with recipe.

Note: Eggplant which is to be stuffed and baked should not be peeled.

To Simmer: Combine eggplant, vinegar, and water to cover in a saucepan; bring to a boil. Reduce heat; cover and simmer 20 minutes or until tender. Drain well; cool slightly, and mash. Add salt and pepper to taste. Yield: 2 to 4 servings.

Other Cooking Methods: Bake; fry; deep-fry.

Serving Suggestions: Eggplant may be served with any of the following: Cheese Sauce, French Dressing, Fresh Tomato Sauce, Mason County Relish, Oil and Lemon sauce, or Hot Pepper Sauce.

BAKED EGGPLANT

4 slices bacon
1 small onion, finely chopped
1 large eggplant, cleaned,
   cooked, and mashed
1 egg, beaten
1 cup soft breadcrumbs
¾ teaspoon salt
⅛ teaspoon pepper

Cook bacon in a medium skillet over low heat until crisp. Remove bacon; reserve drippings in skillet. Crumble bacon; set aside. Sauté onion in drippings until tender.

Combine mashed eggplant, bacon, onion, egg, breadcrumbs, salt, and pepper; mix well. Spoon mixture into a greased 1-quart casserole. Bake, uncovered, at 350° for 1 hour. Yield: 4 servings.

BROILED EGGPLANT

1 large eggplant
Salt
2 tablespoons lemon juice
2 tablespoons olive oil
1 teaspoon dried whole
   dillweed

Peel eggplant, and cut into ½-inch slices. Sprinkle each slice with salt. Let stand 30 minutes; rinse and drain well.

Brush both sides of each slice of eggplant with lemon juice and olive oil; sprinkle with dillweed. Broil eggplant 6 inches from heat about 6 minutes on each side or until lightly browned. Yield: 4 to 6 servings.

EGGPLANT FRITTERS

¼ cup plus 2 tablespoons
   all-purpose flour
1 tablespoon baking powder
¼ teaspoon salt
2 eggs, beaten
1 medium eggplant, cleaned,
   cooked, and mashed
Vegetable oil
Orange marmalade

Combine flour, baking powder, and salt in a medium mixing bowl; stir in eggs. Add mashed eggplant, mixing well.

Carefully drop batter by tablespoonfuls into deep hot oil (375°); cook only a few at a time, turning once. Fry until fritters are a deep golden brown. Drain well on paper towels. Serve fritters with orange marmalade. Yield: about 1 dozen.

George Washington's Fried Eggplant, good as ever.

GEORGE WASHINGTON'S FRIED EGGPLANT

2 small eggplant
Salt
1⅓ cups all-purpose
   flour
1 teaspoon salt
¼ teaspoon pepper
¾ cup milk
2 egg yolks, beaten
1 tablespoon butter
   or margarine,
   melted
Vegetable oil

Peel eggplant, and cut into ½-inch slices. Sprinkle each slice with salt. Let stand 30 minutes; rinse and drain well.

Combine flour, salt, and pepper; add milk, egg yolks, and butter, mixing well. Dip eggplant slices into batter, and fry in hot oil (375°) until golden brown. Drain on paper towels, and serve immediately. Yield: 6 to 8 servings.

OAKLAWN GARDENS' STUFFED EGGPLANT

2 medium eggplant
4 slices bacon
2 medium onions, chopped
1 small green pepper,
   chopped
1 clove garlic, minced
½ pound lean ground beef
1 tablespoon Worcestershire
   sauce
¼ cup chopped fresh parsley
3 slices bread, torn into
   bite-size pieces
½ teaspoon salt
¼ teaspoon pepper
½ cup soft breadcrumbs
2 tablespoons butter or
   margarine, melted

Wash eggplant thoroughly; cook in boiling water to cover 10 minutes or until tender but firm. Drain and cool slightly. Cut each in half lengthwise; remove and reserve pulp, leaving a firm shell.

Cook bacon in a large skillet until crisp; drain bacon well, reserving drippings in skillet. Crumble bacon, and set aside.

Sauté onion, green pepper, and garlic in reserved drippings until tender. Add ground beef and Worcestershire sauce; cook an additional 3 minutes or until beef is browned. Stir in eggplant pulp, bacon, parsley, bread pieces, salt, and pepper; cook until thoroughly heated.

Place eggplant shells in a 12- x 8- x 2-inch baking dish. Spoon eggplant mixture into shells; top with breadcrumbs and butter. Bake at 375° for 20 minutes or until lightly browned. Yield: 4 servings.

N ative to the Mediterranean area, eggplant, as it traveled the trade routes into Europe, enjoyed mixed reviews. First regarded as an ornamental, eggplant came into use in Spain as an aphrodisiac. The English were suspicious of the "mad apple," tarring it with the same brush as the other nightshades. (Carrots weren't eaten either; the foliage was worn in the hair.)

SMOTHERED EGGPLANT WITH SHRIMP

4 green onions, chopped
1 small green pepper,
   chopped
1 clove garlic, minced
3 tablespoons butter or
   margarine
1 large tomato, peeled
   and chopped
1½ cups water
½ teaspoon salt
¼ teaspoon pepper
1 medium eggplant,
   peeled and cubed
½ pound medium
   shrimp, peeled and
   deveined

Sauté onion, green pepper, and garlic in butter in a large skillet until tender. Add tomato, water, salt, and pepper; cover and cook over low heat 15 minutes, stirring occasionally.

Stir in eggplant and shrimp; cook, uncovered, over medium heat 10 minutes. Yield: 4 to 6 servings.

GREENS

HOW TO PREPARE FRESH GREENS

1 bunch collard, mustard, or
   turnip greens
½ pound salt pork, cubed
¼ cup water
1 teaspoon salt

To Clean: Discard any wilted or yellowed leaves and pulpy stems. Washing is the most important part of preparing any greens. Fill both bowls of double sink (or sink and a large pan) with lukewarm water. Wash greens by plunging up and down in one sink; then lift greens out of the water and into the other container of water. Repeat procedure, rinsing sink or pan between washings, until no trace of sand remains in final rinse water.

Note: Greens are not well washed unless lifted out of the water. Simply pulling the plug in the sink or pouring the water from the pan without first removing the greens will not rinse away the sand.

To Simmer: Place greens in a Dutch oven; add salt pork, water, and salt. Cook over low heat until steam begins to form. Cover; reduce heat and simmer, stirring occasionally, 1½ hours or until greens are tender. Add water, if needed. Yield: about 6 to 8 servings.

Serving Suggestions: Fresh greens may be served with any of the following: Basil Vinegar, Chive Blossom Vinegar, Mason County Relish, Oil and Lemon Sauce, or Hot Pepper Sauce.

COLLARD GREENS

1 bunch (about 3 pounds)
   collard greens, cleaned
1 (½-pound) ham hock
1 quart water
1 teaspoon salt
1 teaspoon sugar

Place collards in a large bowl; add water to cover, and set aside for 1 hour. Drain well.

Wash ham hock; place in a large Dutch oven. Add remaining ingredients; bring to a boil. Add collard greens, stirring well. Reduce heat; cover and simmer 2 hours or until greens are tender. Yield: 6 to 8 servings.

OCRACOKE COLLARDS

1 bunch (about 3½ pounds)
   collard greens, cleaned
½ pound salt pork, cubed
1 teaspoon salt
4 medium potatoes, peeled
   and quartered

Place collard greens, salt pork, salt, and water to cover in a large Dutch oven; bring to a boil. Reduce heat; cover and simmer 1½ hours. Add potatoes; cover and simmer an additional 30 minutes or until potatoes are tender. Yield: 6 to 8 servings.

Aerial view of Ocracoke Island, North Carolina.

LOUISIANA MUSTARD GREENS

2 bunches (about 4 pounds)
 mustard greens, cleaned
1½ quarts water
4 slices bacon
Vegetable oil
¼ cup all-purpose flour
1 medium onion, chopped
1 small green pepper,
 chopped
1 teaspoon salt
¼ teaspoon pepper

Place mustard greens in a large Dutch oven. Add water, and bring to a boil. Reduce heat, and simmer 15 minutes; drain. Set aside.

Cook bacon until crisp, reserving drippings. Crumble bacon, and set aside.

Add oil to reserved drippings to yield ¼ cup; pour into a large skillet. Add flour, mixing well; cook over medium heat, stirring constantly, 10 minutes or until roux is the color of a copper penny. Add onion; sauté 3 minutes or until tender. Stir in mustard greens, green pepper, salt, and pepper. Cover and simmer 1 hour. Stir in reserved bacon. Yield: 8 to 10 servings.

MUSTARD GREENS AND TURNIPS

2 bunches (about 4 pounds)
 mustard greens, cleaned
4 medium turnips, peeled and
 quartered
1 medium onion, chopped
2 tablespoons vegetable oil
1 teaspoon salt
1 teaspoon sugar
½ teaspoon pepper

Place mustard greens and remaining ingredients in a large Dutch oven; add water to cover. Bring to a boil; reduce heat and simmer, uncovered, for 2 hours or until mustard greens are tender. Yield: 8 to 10 servings.

SOUTHERN-STYLE MUSTARD GREENS

1 (½-pound) ham hock
2 quarts water
2 medium onions, peeled and
 quartered
1 small red pepper pod
1 bunch (about 2 pounds)
 mustard greens, cleaned
1 teaspoon salt
1 medium onion, sliced and
 separated into rings
2 hard-cooked eggs, finely
 grated

Wash ham hock, and place in a 10-quart Dutch oven. Add water, onions, and pepper pod; bring to a boil. Reduce heat, and simmer 1 hour or until meat is tender.

Add mustard greens and salt to Dutch oven; bring to a boil. Cover; reduce heat and simmer 2 hours or until greens are tender. Drain, reserving 1½ cups pot likker. Remove pepper pod; discard.

Transfer mustard greens to a serving dish. Pour pot likker over top, and garnish with onion rings and grated egg. Yield: 4 to 6 servings.

TURNIP GREENS IN "POT LIKKER"

½ pound salt pork, cubed
2 quarts water
2 medium onions, peeled and
 quartered
1 small red pepper pod
2 bunches (about 6 pounds)
 turnip greens, cleaned
1½ teaspoons salt

Wash salt pork, and place in a 10-quart Dutch oven. Add water, onions, and pepper pod; bring to a boil. Reduce heat, and simmer 2 hours or until meat is tender.

Add turnip greens and salt to Dutch oven; bring to a boil. Cover; reduce heat and simmer 2 hours or until turnip greens are tender. Drain, reserving pot likker to serve over turnip greens, if desired. Remove pepper pod; discard. Yield: 12 to 14 servings.

"After having greens for the noonday meal, reheat the pot likker Put a piece of cornbread in individual bowls, and pour the pot likker over the cornbread. Eat with a spoon."

Heart-of-Texas Cookbook

TURNIP GREENS AND CORNMEAL DUMPLINGS

1 (½-pound) ham hock
2 quarts water
1 bunch (about 3 pounds)
 turnip greens with roots,
 cleaned
1 teaspoon salt
1 cup cornmeal
½ teaspoon salt
1 cup boiling water
1 egg, beaten
All-purpose flour

Wash ham hock, and place in an 8-quart Dutch oven; add water, and bring to a boil. Reduce heat, and simmer 1 hour or until meat is tender.

Peel turnip roots, and cut in half. Add turnip greens, turnip roots, and 1 teaspoon salt to Dutch oven; bring to a boil. Cover; reduce heat and simmer 2 hours or until greens and roots are tender.

Combine cornmeal and ½ teaspoon salt; mix well. Stir in boiling water. Add egg, and mix well. Drop cornmeal mixture by tablespoonfuls onto a well-floured board, and roll in flour. Place dumplings over hot turnip greens; cover and cook over medium heat 15 minutes. Serve immediately with turnip greens and pot likker. Yield: 8 to 10 servings.

Turnip Greens with Cornmeal Dumplings will be the making of a down-home dinner. To tell the truth, it is a meal in itself with turnips and pork in it.

VARIETY GREENS

KALE SALAD GREENS

1 (½-pound) ham hock
2 medium onions, peeled and quartered
1 small red pepper pod
2 quarts water
2 bunches (about 3 pounds) kale
1 medium onion, thinly sliced
2 hard-cooked eggs, thinly sliced

Wash ham hock, and place in an 8-quart Dutch oven. Add quartered onion, pepper pod, and water; bring to a boil. Reduce heat, and simmer 2 hours or until meat is tender.

Check kale carefully; remove pulpy stems and discolored spots on leaves. Wash kale thoroughly; drain well. Chop kale leaves.

Add kale to Dutch oven; bring to a boil. Cover, reduce heat, and simmer 2 hours or until kale is tender. Remove pepper pod; discard. Spoon kale into a serving dish; garnish with onion and egg slices. Yield: 8 to 10 servings.

BRAISED LETTUCE

2 large heads romaine lettuce
1 teaspoon salt
2 tablespoons butter
2 tablespoons all-purpose flour
1 cup chicken broth
2 tablespoons whipping cream
1 teaspoon lemon juice
¼ teaspoon salt
Dash of pepper
2 tablespoons grated Parmesan cheese

Separate lettuce leaves, and wash thoroughly. Tear into bite-size pieces. Place lettuce and water to cover in a large Dutch oven; set aside 1 hour. Drain.

Place lettuce, 1 cup water, and salt in a Dutch oven. Bring to a boil. Cover; reduce heat, and simmer 20 minutes. Drain well.

Melt butter in a heavy saucepan over low heat; stir in flour. Cook 1 minute, stirring constantly. Gradually add broth; cook over medium heat, stirring constantly, until thickened and bubbly. Add cream; cook 1 minute, stirring constantly. Stir in lemon juice, salt, and pepper. Pour sauce over cooked lettuce. Sprinkle cheese over top. Yield: 4 servings.

FIELD CRESS

1 pound field cress
2 cups water
1 (¼-pound) ham hock

Remove tough stems from field cress. Wash and pat leaves dry. Place field cress, water, and ham hock in a small Dutch oven. Bring to a boil; reduce heat. Cover and cook over low heat 25 minutes. Drain well. Yield: about 2 servings.

POKE SALLET WITH BACON

3 pounds fresh, young poke shoots
3 quarts water, divided
¾ teaspoon salt
5 slices bacon
2 tablespoons bacon drippings

Check poke shoots carefully; remove pulpy stems and discolored spots on leaves. Wash poke shoots thoroughly; drain well. Tear poke into bite-size pieces.

Place poke shoots, 2 quarts water, and salt in an 8-quart Dutch oven. Bring to a boil; cover and cook over medium heat 25 minutes. Drain well.

Sauté poke and bacon in bacon drippings 15 minutes.

Place sautéed poke and bacon in a Dutch oven with 1 quart water. Bring to a boil. Cover; reduce heat and simmer for 1½ hours or until poke is tender. Yield: 4 servings.

Curly dark kale is one of the most flavorful members of the cabbage family, as in this dish of Kale Salad Greens.

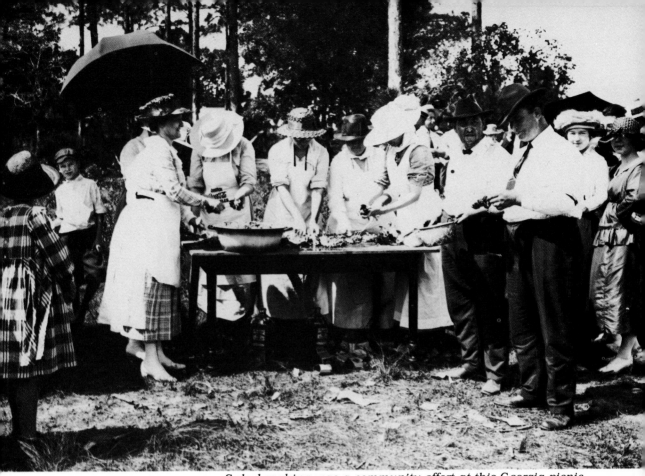

Salad-making was a community effort at this Georgia picnic.

ARKANSAS POKE GREENS

1½ pounds fresh, young poke shoots
8 slices bacon
6 eggs, beaten
Salt and pepper to taste

Check poke shoots carefully; remove pulpy stems and discolored spots on leaves. Wash leaves thoroughly; drain well.

Place poke shoots and water to cover in an 8-quart Dutch oven; bring to a boil. Cover; reduce heat and simmer 30 minutes or until poke is tender. Drain well and chop. Set aside.

Cook bacon in a medium skillet over low heat until crisp. Drain bacon; reserve 3 tablespoons drippings in skillet. Crumble bacon. Add chopped poke and bacon to bacon drippings; cook over medium heat 15 minutes, stirring frequently.

Stir in eggs; cook over medium heat, stirring often, until eggs are firm but still moist. Add salt and pepper to taste. Yield: 4 servings.

POKE SALLET

3 pounds fresh, young poke shoots
Salt and pepper to taste

Check poke shoots carefully; remove pulpy stems and discolored spots on leaves. Wash poke shoots thoroughly; drain well. Tear poke into bite-size pieces.

Place poke shoots and water to cover in a Dutch oven; bring to a boil. Cover; reduce heat and simmer 45 minutes or until poke shoots are tender. Drain; add salt and pepper to taste. Yield: about 4 servings.

Serving Suggestions: Poke Sallet may be served with Drawn Butter or Lemon-Butter Sauce.

Avoid pokeweed six to eight feet high; the roots and berries are poisonous. But go back in the spring when the poke shoots are up just a few inches. They are now just right for the pot. Cook poke shoots as you would asparagus, with steam. When the leaves are still small, Southerners like to mix them with other wild greens, cook them with salt pork, and serve them up with plenty of pot likker and cornbread. It is an unbeatable old-time combination. The term sallet is a variation of salad, but in the South it means greens, as in "a mess of."

Sautéed Swiss Chard served with bacon and vinegar.

SAUTÉED SWISS CHARD

2 pounds fresh Swiss chard
6 slices bacon
1 tablespoon vinegar

Remove stalks and tough stems from Swiss chard. Wash leaves thoroughly, and tear into bite-size pieces.

Place in a Dutch oven (do not add water); cover and cook over medium heat 4 to 6 minutes or until tender. Drain well.

Cook bacon in a large skillet until crisp; drain on paper towels. Crumble and set aside, reserving drippings in skillet.

Add Swiss chard to skillet; cook over medium heat 4 to 5 minutes, stirring occasionally. Transfer to a serving dish. Sprinkle with vinegar and bacon. Yield: 2 to 4 servings.

CREAMED SWISS CHARD

3 pounds fresh Swiss chard
1 tablespoon all-purpose flour
3 tablespoons butter or margarine, melted
1 cup whipping cream
¼ teaspoon salt
⅛ teaspoon pepper
¼ teaspoon ground nutmeg

Remove stalks and tough stems from Swiss chard. Wash thoroughly, and tear into large pieces.

Place Swiss chard in a large Dutch oven (do not add water). Cover and cook over medium heat 4 to 6 minutes or until tender. Drain; place on paper towels, and squeeze until barely moist. Return Swiss chard to Dutch oven.

Melt butter in a small saucepan over low heat; add flour, and stir until smooth. Add to Swiss chard, stirring well. Add whipping cream; cook over low heat 15 minutes or until mixture is slightly thickened, stirring occasionally. Add salt, pepper, and ground nutmeg; stir well. Serve immediately. Yield: 4 servings.

While chard is a near relative of the beet, its root is not the edible part. Leaves and stems may be used separately, the leaves steamed like spinach, and the stems prepared like asparagus. Serve stems with hollandaise or butter sauce. Chard does not ship well; wilted leaves and coarse stems mean an overaged vegetable.

STEAMED SWISS CHARD

3 pounds fresh Swiss chard
Salt to taste

Remove stalks and tough stems from Swiss chard; wash leaves thoroughly, and tear into bite-size pieces.

Place in a Dutch oven (do not add water); cover and cook over medium heat 4 to 6 minutes or until tender. Drain well; add salt to taste. Yield: 4 servings.

Serving Suggestion: Swiss Chard may be served with Oil and Lemon Sauce.

LEEKS

HOW TO PREPARE FRESH LEEKS

12 large leeks (about 4½ pounds)
2 tablespoons butter or margarine, melted
Salt and pepper to taste

To Clean: Discard outer leaves; cut off root and cut top leaves to where dark green begins to pale. Wash carefully under cold running water to remove grit. Leeks may be prepared whole, sliced in half, or cut into pieces as directed in recipe.

To Boil: Cook leeks in boiling water to cover 15 minutes or until tender. Drain well. Arrange on serving dish. Pour melted butter over leeks, and sprinkle with salt and pepper to taste. Yield: 8 servings.

Other Cooking Methods: Braise in chicken broth; steam.

Serving Suggestions: Leeks may be served with any of the following: Cheese Sauce, Fresh Tomato Sauce, or any hollandaise, sour cream, or white sauce. Chilled cooked leeks may be served with salads.

William Bartram, the Philadelphia Quaker who was the first great American-born natural scientist, fared extensively throughout the Carolinas, Georgia, and Florida. He published his *Travels* in 1791. Already, in his poetic, prophetic imagination, he could see how the Deep South, under "the culture of industrious planters and mechanics, would in a little time exhibit other scenes than it does at present, delightful as it is, for by the arts of agriculture and commerce, almost every desirable thing in life might be produced and made plentiful here, and thereby establish a rich, populous, and delightful region; as this soil and climate appear to be of a favourable nature for the production of almost all the fruits of the earth . . . corn, rice, and all the esculent vegetables. . . . "

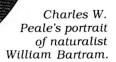

Free Library of Philadelphia

Charles W. Peale's portrait of naturalist William Bartram.

Leeks and New Potatoes. Welshmen tuck leeks into their hats on St. David's Day, a patriotic gesture.

CREAMED LEEKS

8 large leeks (about 3
   pounds), cleaned
¼ cup butter or margarine,
   divided
2 tablespoons all-purpose
   flour
1 cup milk
½ teaspoon salt
¼ teaspoon pepper

Cut cleaned leeks into 2-inch pieces, and place in a large heavy skillet; cover and cook in a small amount of boiling water 30 minutes or until tender. Drain. Rinse quickly with cold water; drain well. Transfer leeks to a serving dish, and set aside. Keep warm.

Melt 2 tablespoons butter in a heavy saucepan over low heat; add flour, stirring until smooth. Cook 1 minute, stirring constantly. Gradually add milk; cook over medium heat, stirring constantly, until sauce is thickened and bubbly. Stir in remaining 2 tablespoons butter, salt, and pepper. Pour sauce over prepared leeks. Serve immediately. Yield: 6 servings.

BRAISED LEEKS

¼ cup butter or margarine
8 large leeks (about 3
   pounds), cleaned
1 cup water
½ teaspoon salt
¼ teaspoon pepper

Melt butter in a large heavy skillet; add leeks, tossing well to coat with butter. Cover and cook over medium heat 10 minutes. Add water; bring to a boil. Reduce heat; cover and cook over low heat 15 minutes or until leeks are tender. Drain well. Sprinkle with salt and pepper. Yield: 6 servings.

LEEKS AND NEW POTATOES

10 new potatoes
3 large leeks (about 1½
   pounds), cleaned
3 cups water
¼ pound salt pork
1 teaspoon maple syrup
Salt to taste

Wash potatoes; pare a 1-inch strip around center of each potato. Cut leeks into 2-inch pieces.

Combine potatoes, leeks, water, salt pork, and maple syrup in a medium Dutch oven. Bring to a boil; cover. Reduce heat, and simmer 25 minutes or until potatoes and leeks are tender. Add salt to taste. Yield: 6 servings.

LEEKS WITH TOMATOES

6 large leeks (about 2
   pounds), cleaned
½ cup chopped onion
½ cup chopped celery
2 tablespoons olive
   oil
1 cup chopped fresh tomato
1 tablespoon chopped
   fresh parsley
½ teaspoon salt
⅛ teaspoon pepper
¼ teaspoon dried whole
   dillweed

Cut leeks into 1-inch pieces, and set aside.

Sauté onion and celery in olive oil in a heavy skillet over medium heat until tender. Add leeks and remaining ingredients; stir well. Cover and cook over low heat 25 minutes or until leeks are tender. Yield: 4 servings.

MUSHROOMS

HOW TO PREPARE FRESH MUSHROOMS

1 pound fresh mushrooms
¼ cup butter
Salt and pepper to taste

To Clean: There is every reason for washing mushrooms, and only one reason for not doing so: the gills absorb water. You may clean them with a damp cloth or a mushroom brush. Or take the route of many professional cooks and wash them in a large pan of cool water into which you have swished a handful of flour. With a rapid hand-washing movement, rub mushrooms lightly against one another, immediately place them in a cloth towel, and dry them quickly. Trim base of stems. Mushrooms may be prepared whole using the caps and chopping the stems, or they may be thinly sliced.

To Sauté: Melt butter in a large skillet over medium heat; add mushrooms and cook, uncovered, 8 minutes or until tender, stirring frequently. (If mushrooms are sliced, cook 4 minutes or until tender.) Add salt and pepper to taste. Serve immediately. Yield: 4 servings.

Other Cooking Methods: Broil; deep-fry; stuff and bake.

Serving Suggestions: Sautéed mushrooms may be served with Drawn Butter, French Dressing, Lemon-Butter Sauce, or Oil and Lemon Sauce.

BROILED MUSHROOMS

12 large fresh mushrooms, cleaned
2 tablespoons butter or margarine, softened
¼ teaspoon garlic powder
12 slices bread, cut into 2½-inch rounds and toasted
Chopped fresh parsley

Remove mushroom stems, and reserve for another recipe. Place mushroom caps, top side down, in a shallow baking dish.

Combine butter and garlic powder; blend well. Dot each mushroom with butter mixture.

Broil 4 inches from heat about 5 minutes. Place on toast rounds, and garnish with parsley. Serve immediately. Yield: 12 servings.

BROILED STUFFED MUSHROOMS

24 large fresh mushrooms, cleaned
½ pound bulk pork sausage
1 cup soft breadcrumbs
¼ teaspoon salt
Dash of pepper

Remove mushroom stems; chop and set aside. Reserve mushroom caps.

Brown sausage in a skillet, stirring to crumble; drain. Combine sausage, mushroom stems, breadcrumbs, salt, and pepper; mix well. Spoon into mushroom caps.

Place stuffed mushrooms in a lightly greased 13- x 9- x 2-inch baking dish. Broil 6 inches from heat 5 minutes or just until breadcrumbs are lightly browned. Yield: 12 servings.

CREAMED MUSHROOMS

2 tablespoons butter
¼ cup all-purpose flour
½ pound fresh mushrooms, cleaned
1 cup milk
1 teaspoon salt
⅛ teaspoon pepper
6 slices bread, toasted
Paprika

Melt butter in a heavy skillet over low heat. Add flour; cook 5 minutes, stirring constantly. Add mushrooms, and stir gently; cover and cook 5 minutes. Gradually add milk, stirring until smooth. Add salt and pepper; cook over medium heat, stirring occasionally, until thickened and bubbly. Spoon mixture over toast; sprinkle with paprika. Yield: 6 servings.

Broiled Stuffed Mushrooms (rear) and Creamed Mushrooms to serve over toast.

BAKED STUFFED MUSHROOMS

1 pound large fresh
  mushrooms, cleaned
2 tablespoons butter or
  margarine
¼ pound ground veal
¼ cup chopped onion
1 clove garlic, minced
1 tablespoon chopped
  fresh parsley
½ teaspoon celery salt
¼ teaspoon pepper
Sauce (recipe follows)

Remove stems from mushrooms; chop stems. Set mushroom caps aside.

Melt butter in a heavy skillet. Add chopped stems, veal, onion, and garlic; sauté mixture until veal is browned, stirring to crumble. Add seasonings; mix well. Drain off pan drippings.

Spoon mixture into mushroom caps; place caps in a lightly greased 13- x 9- x 2-inch baking dish. Bake at 375° for 20 minutes. Spoon sauce over mushrooms to serve. Yield: 10 to 12 appetizer servings.

Sauce:

¼ cup finely chopped onion
2 tablespoons butter or
  margarine
1 tablespoon plus 1½
  teaspoons all-purpose flour
½ teaspoon marjoram leaves,
  crushed
½ teaspoon celery salt
¼ teaspoon dry mustard
1 tablespoon lemon juice
1 teaspoon Worcestershire
  sauce
½ cup Sauterne or other
  white wine
½ cup commercial sour
  cream

Sauté onion in butter until tender. Add flour, stirring until onion is coated. Add marjoram, celery salt, and mustard. Cook 1 minute, stirring constantly. Gradually add lemon juice, Worcestershire sauce, and wine. Cook over medium heat, stirring constantly, until thickened.

Remove from heat; add sour cream. Cook until thoroughly heated. Yield: about 1½ cups.

Churchill Downs clubhouse veranda, 1914 Kentucky Derby.

SHERRIED MUSHROOMS

1 pound fresh mushrooms,
  cleaned
½ cup water
2 tablespoons butter or
  margarine
2 tablespoons all-purpose
  flour
½ cup chicken broth
¼ teaspoon salt
⅛ teaspoon pepper
2 tablespoons sherry

Place mushrooms on a lightly greased 15- x 10- x 1-inch jellyroll pan. Add water. Bake at 275° for 30 minutes. Transfer mushrooms to a serving dish; reserve liquid in pan.

Melt butter in a small saucepan over low heat. Add flour; stir until smooth. Cook 1 minute, stirring constantly. Gradually add chicken broth and reserved liquid; cook over medium heat, stirring constantly, until thickened and bubbly. Stir in salt, pepper, and sherry. Pour sauce over mushrooms. Yield: 6 to 8 servings.

CHURCHILL DOWNS SAUTÉED FRESH MUSHROOMS

½ cup butter
1 pound fresh mushrooms,
  cleaned
1 tablespoon Worcestershire
  sauce
½ teaspoon garlic salt
6 slices bread, toasted

Melt butter in a large skillet. Add mushrooms, Worcestershire sauce, and garlic salt. Cook over low heat, stirring frequently, 8 minutes or until mushrooms are tender. Serve hot over toasted bread. Yield: 6 servings.

Fresh mushrooms under lattice crust in Mushroom Pie.

MUSHROOM PIE

Lattice-Crust Pastry
1½ pounds small fresh
  mushrooms, cleaned
1 large onion, chopped
¼ cup plus 2 tablespoons
  butter or margarine,
  divided
3 tablespoons all-purpose
  flour
½ cup chicken broth
2 tablespoons Madeira or
  other sweet wine
½ teaspoon salt
½ teaspoon celery salt
⅛ teaspoon pepper
Dash of red pepper

Prepare Lattice-Crust Pastry; set aside.

Sauté mushrooms and onion in ¼ cup butter in a large skillet 8 minutes or until vegetables are tender. Set aside.

Melt remaining butter in a small saucepan over low heat. Add flour, stirring until smooth. Cook 1 minute, stirring constantly. Gradually add broth and wine; cook over medium heat, stirring constantly, until thickened and bubbly. Stir in salt and pepper. Combine sauce, sautéed mushrooms, and onion; stir well.

Spoon mushroom mixture into pastry shell. Arrange pastry strips in lattice design over filling; seal edges and flute. Bake at 375° for 40 minutes or until browned. Yield: 6 to 8 servings.

Serving Suggestion: Mushroom Pie is an excellent side dish to serve with beef.

Lattice-Crust Pastry:

2 cups all-purpose flour
½ teaspoon salt
⅔ cup plus 2 tablespoons
  shortening
5 to 6 tablespoons cold water

Combine flour and salt; cut in shortening with a pastry blender until mixture resembles coarse meal. Sprinkle cold water evenly over surface; stir with a fork until all ingredients are moistened. Divide dough in half, and roll each portion to ⅛-inch thickness on a lightly floured surface.

Carefully fit one portion into a 9-inch pieplate and set aside. Cut remaining portion into 14 (¾-inch-wide) strips. Yield: pastry for one lattice-crust 9-inch pie.

MUSHROOM STROGANOFF

1 pound fresh mushrooms,
  cleaned
½ cup chopped onion
¼ cup butter or margarine
½ teaspoon salt
¼ teaspoon pepper
1 tablespoon all-purpose flour
¼ cup milk
¾ cup commercial sour
  cream
½ teaspoon Worcestershire
  sauce
Toast points
Chopped fresh parsley

Remove mushroom stems; chop stems. Sauté mushroom caps, chopped stems, and onion in butter in a large skillet until vegetables are tender. Stir in salt and pepper. Reduce heat; cover and simmer 5 minutes.

Combine flour and milk, stirring well. Stir milk mixture into mushroom mixture; cook over medium heat until bubbly. Remove from heat; add sour cream and Worcestershire sauce, stirring well. Cook over low heat until thoroughly heated. Serve hot over toast points and garnish with parsley. Yield: 4 to 6 servings.

MUSHROOM PAPRIKA

3 medium onions,
  chopped
3 tablespoons butter or
  margarine
1½ pounds fresh
  mushrooms, cleaned
  and sliced
1½ cups chicken broth
2 teaspoons paprika
¼ teaspoon salt
½ teaspoon pepper
Mashed potatoes (optional)
Hot cooked rice (optional)

Sauté onion in butter in a large skillet until tender; add remaining ingredients, stirring well. Cook over medium heat, stirring occasionally, 15 minutes or until mushrooms are tender. Serve over mashed potatoes or hot cooked rice, if desired. Yield: 6 to 8 servings.

OKRA

HOW TO PREPARE FRESH OKRA

1 pound fresh okra
½ teaspoon salt
2 tablespoons butter or margarine, melted
1 tablespoon lemon juice

To Clean: Use only fresh pods 2 to 4 inches long. Tender okra will snap easily; old pods are dull and woody. Wash okra; remove stems, and slice as directed in recipe.

Note: When cooking whole okra, leave a small portion of stem for a firmer texture.

To Boil: Place whole okra, salt, and water to cover in a large saucepan. Bring to a boil. Reduce heat; cover, and simmer 10 minutes or until tender. Drain. Stir in butter and lemon juice. Yield: 4 servings.

Other Cooking Methods: Steam whole; cut crosswise, and batter and fry or deep-fry.

Serving Suggestions: Okra may be served with Drawn Butter, Fresh Tomato Sauce, or Lemon-Butter Sauce.

PAN-FRIED OKRA

1 pound okra, cleaned
¾ cup cornmeal
½ teaspoon salt
Vegetable oil

Cut okra crosswise into ½-inch slices; set aside.

Combine cornmeal and salt, mixing well. Dredge sliced okra in cornmeal mixture. Cook in ½ inch oil over high heat until lightly browned, stirring occasionally. Drain on paper towels, and serve immediately. Yield: 4 servings.

Okra vendors in New Orleans' French Market, from a sketch by A. Waud.

Okra and Tomatoes, an old favorite in the South.

BATTER-FRIED OKRA

1 pound small okra, cleaned
1 teaspoon salt
¼ teaspoon pepper
2½ cups fine, dry breadcrumbs
4 eggs, beaten
Vegetable oil

Combine okra and water to cover in a medium saucepan. Bring to a boil. Reduce heat; cover and simmer 5 minutes. Drain well.

Sprinkle okra with salt and pepper. Roll each piece in breadcrumbs. Dip in egg; roll in breadcrumbs.

Deep fry okra in hot oil (375°) until golden brown. Drain well on paper towels. Yield: 4 to 6 servings.

Serving Suggestions: Batter-Fried Okra may be served with Dill Sauce, Horseradish Sauce, or Mustard Dip Sauce.

OKRA AND TOMATOES

2 pounds okra, cleaned
1 medium onion, chopped
¼ cup chopped green pepper
2 tablespoons vegetable oil
1 (14½-ounce) can whole tomatoes, undrained
1 tablespoon vinegar
1 teaspoon salt
⅛ teaspoon pepper

Cut okra crosswise into ½-inch slices, and set aside.

Sauté onion and green pepper in oil in a heavy skillet over medium heat until tender. Add tomatoes, vinegar, salt, and pepper; stir well. Cover and cook over low heat 5 minutes. Add sliced okra; cover and simmer 1 hour. Yield: about 8 servings.

BAKED OKRA

1 pound okra, cleaned
1 large onion, chopped
1 medium-size green pepper, chopped
2 tablespoons bacon drippings
¾ teaspoon salt
⅛ teaspoon pepper
4 slices bacon

Cut okra crosswise into ½-inch slices. Sauté okra, onion, and green pepper in bacon drippings in a large skillet 5 minutes or until vegetables are tender. Stir in salt and pepper.

Spoon okra mixture into a 9-inch pieplate. Top with bacon slices. Bake at 350° for 30 minutes. Yield: 6 servings.

OKRA CROQUETTES

1½ cups cleaned and sliced okra (about ¾ pound)
1½ cups cooked rice
1 cup chopped tomato
¾ cup chopped onion
1 tablespoon sugar
1½ teaspoons salt
1 teaspoon baking powder
¾ teaspoon pepper
2 eggs, beaten
1 cup cornmeal
1 cup all-purpose flour
Vegetable oil

Chop okra slices. Combine chopped okra, rice, tomato, onion, sugar, salt, baking powder, and pepper. Stir in beaten eggs. Add cornmeal and flour, mixing well.

Drop mixture by tablespoonfuls into deep hot oil (375°). Cook 1 minute or until golden brown, turning as necessary. Drain on paper towels. Serve hot. Yield: about 3 dozen.

Serving Suggestions: Okra Croquettes may be served with Dill Sauce, Horseradish Sauce, Mustard Dip Sauce, or any sour cream sauce.

OKRA PILAU

3 slices bacon, diced
3 cups cleaned and thinly sliced okra (about 1½ pounds)
1 cup chopped onion
¾ cup chopped green pepper
1 cup uncooked regular rice
2 cups chicken broth
1 (16-ounce) can whole tomatoes, drained and chopped
1 teaspoon salt

Sauté bacon and okra in a Dutch oven until lightly browned. Add onion and green pepper; cook over low heat, stirring constantly, until tender.

Stir in rice, broth, tomatoes, and salt. Bring to a boil; stir once. Reduce heat; cover and simmer 15 minutes or until all liquid is absorbed. Before serving, fluff lightly with a fork. Yield: 8 to 10 servings.

ONIONS

Courtesy of Munson-Williams-Proctor Institute, Utica, New York

HOW TO PREPARE FRESH ONIONS

4 large onions

To Peel: Hold onion under cool tap water when peeling to keep down the oils that cause tears. Cut a slice from top and root end of onion; remove outer skin. Onions may be cooked whole or sliced into rings as directed in recipe.

To Parboil: Place onions in saucepan, and add salted water to cover; bring to a boil. Reduce heat; cover and cook 10 minutes. Drain. (Parboiling onions helps to reduce strong flavor.)

To Boil: Place parboiled onions in a saucepan; cover with boiling water. Reduce heat, and cook 1 hour or until tender. Drain. Yield: 4 servings.

Other Cooking Methods: Batter and deep-fry; sauté; steam; to use raw in salads, crisp rings in ice water.

Serving Suggestions: Boiled onions may be served with melted butter and seasonings to taste or with any of the following: Cheese Sauce, Drawn Butter, any herb butter or spread, or any white sauce.

English-born artist Angélique (Lilly) Martin Spencer came to America at age 8. Critics praised her talent for making everyday matters come alive as art.

Peeling Onions

George Washington stops to chat with a farm hand during a daily tour of his estate at Mount Vernon.

GEORGE WASHINGTON'S GLAZED ONIONS

1½ pounds boiling onions, peeled
3 tablespoons butter or margarine
½ cup firmly packed brown sugar
¼ cup corn syrup
⅛ teaspoon salt

Arrange onions on steaming rack. Place over boiling water; cover and steam 20 minutes or until tender. Place in a greased 8-inch square baking dish; set aside.

Melt butter over low heat in a medium saucepan. Add sugar, syrup, and salt; bring to a boil. Reduce heat, and simmer 5 minutes without stirring.

Pour glaze over onions; cover and bake at 350° for 45 minutes. Yield: about 4 servings.

At George Washington's Mount Vernon estate, the kitchen garden yielded French artichokes, cucumbers, cauliflower, peas, bush lima beans, turnips, peppers, asparagus, summer squash, rhubarb, parsnips, cabbage, potatoes, beets, and onions. Washington thought of himself as a professional husbandman. "...To see plants rise from the earth and flourish by the superior skill and bounty of the laborer fills a contemplative mind with ideas which are more easy to be conceived than expressed."

BAKED CURRIED ONIONS

2 medium onions, peeled, sliced, and parboiled
2 tablespoons butter or margarine
2 tablespoons all-purpose flour
¼ cup chicken broth
½ cup milk
¼ teaspoon salt
¼ teaspoon red pepper
¼ teaspoon curry powder
¼ teaspoon paprika
¼ cup (1 ounce) shredded sharp Cheddar cheese

Place onion slices in a lightly greased 1-quart casserole, and set aside.

Melt butter in a heavy saucepan over low heat; add flour, stirring until smooth. Cook 1 minute, stirring constantly. Gradually add chicken broth and milk; cook over medium heat, stirring constantly, until thickened and bubbly. Add salt, pepper, curry powder, paprika, and cheese; stir until cheese melts. Spoon mixture over sliced onions. Bake, uncovered, at 350° for 30 minutes. Yield: 4 to 6 servings.

A 1925 picture of little Geraldine White with some mammoth onions. Not for use in these recipes!

ONIONS AU GRATIN

12 medium onions, peeled
¼ cup plus 2 tablespoons butter or margarine, divided
¼ cup plus 2 tablespoons all-purpose flour
2 cups milk
½ teaspoon salt
1 cup (4 ounces) shredded sharp Cheddar cheese
1 cup soft breadcrumbs
½ cup chopped almonds, toasted

Cut a ¼-inch slice from the top of each onion. Reserve slices for use in another recipe.

Cover and cook onions in boiling salted water 30 minutes or until tender but not mushy. Drain, and place in a lightly greased 13- x 9- x 2-inch baking dish; set aside.

Melt ¼ cup butter in a heavy saucepan over low heat; add flour, stirring until smooth. Cook 1 minute, stirring constantly. Gradually add milk; cook over medium heat, stirring constantly, until thickened and bubbly. Add salt and cheese, stirring until cheese melts. Pour cheese sauce over onions.

Melt remaining butter; toss with breadcrumbs. Sprinkle buttered breadcrumbs and toasted almonds over onions. Bake at 350° for 15 minutes or until lightly browned. Yield: 12 servings.

LOUIS SMITH'S SOUTHERN FRIED ONIONS

2 tablespoons bacon drippings
3 large onions, peeled and thinly sliced
1 teaspoon salt
⅛ teaspoon pepper

Heat bacon drippings in a large skillet over medium-high heat. Add onions, salt, and pepper. Cook, stirring frequently, 5 minutes or until onions are tender and lightly browned. Yield: 4 to 6 servings.

Serving Suggestions: Southern Fried Onions may be served as an accompaniment to fried liver, hamburgers, or mashed potatoes.

FRENCH FRIED ONION RINGS

3 large onions, peeled
2 cups milk
1 egg
2 cups all-purpose flour
Vegetable oil
Salt to taste

Cut onions into ¼-inch slices, and separate into rings.

Combine milk and egg; beat well. Dip onion rings in milk mixture; dredge in flour. Repeat procedure with remaining onion to yield a thick coating on each ring.

Fry onion rings in deep hot oil (375°) for 3 to 5 minutes or until golden. Drain well on paper towels. Sprinkle with salt to taste. Yield: 4 servings.

Serving Suggestions: French Fried Onion Rings may be served with any of the following: Dill Sauce, Horseradish Sauce, Mustard Dip Sauce, or any sour cream sauce.

GREEN ONION PIE

3 bunches green onions,
 sliced
¼ cup plus 2 tablespoons
 butter or margarine
1 unbaked 9-inch pastry shell
4 eggs, beaten
1 cup whipping cream
¾ teaspoon salt
⅛ teaspoon pepper

Sauté onion in butter until
tender. Spoon into pastry shell.

Combine eggs, cream, salt,
and pepper; stir well. Pour over
onions. Bake at 425° for 20 minutes or until a knife inserted in
center comes out clean. Let
stand 5 minutes before serving.
Yield: one 9-inch pie.

OKLAHOMA ONION AND EGGS

2 tablespoons bacon
 drippings
½ cup water
1 cup chopped green onion
1 teaspoon salt
12 eggs, beaten

Heat bacon drippings and
water in a large skillet. Add
onion and salt. Cover, and cook
over medium heat 10 minutes
or until tender.

Add eggs; cook over medium
heat, stirring often, until eggs
are firm but still moist. Yield: 6
to 8 servings.

*From 1914 seed catalogue,
a giant Gibralter onion.*

BURPEE'S
GIGANTIC GIBRALTAR
ONION.

INTRODUCED BY US NINETEEN
YEARS AGO THIS HAS PROVED
EACH SEASON AT FORDHOOK FARMS
THE LARGEST OF ALL ONIONS.

The "official" Vidalia
onion (sanctioned by
the Vidalia, Georgia,
Chamber of Commerce) is
grown only within a 30-mile
radius of the town. Similar
onions are grown in other
areas but without the stamp
of approval of the place of ori-
gin. Sweet as an orange with
natural sugar, the Vidalia is
quite perishable. Vidalias
cannot be shipped very long
distances and must be
stored in a cool, dry place,
not touching one another.

STUFFED VIDALIA ONIONS

6 large Vidalia onions, peeled
½ cup butter or margarine
1 cup chopped pitted ripe
 olives
1 cup soft breadcrumbs
¾ cup (3 ounces) shredded
 sharp Cheddar cheese
2 tablespoons chopped fresh
 parsley
¼ teaspoon salt
¼ teaspoon poultry seasoning
¼ teaspoon rubbed sage
Dash of pepper
Paprika

Cut a ¼-inch slice from top
and bottom of each onion, reserving slices. Place onions in a
Dutch oven; add water to cover.
Bring to a boil. Reduce heat;
cover, and simmer 20 minutes
or until tender. Drain and cool.

Chop reserved onion slices;
sauté in butter until tender.
Add next 8 ingredients.

Scoop out center portion of
each onion; discard. Fill each
onion with olive mixture; sprinkle with paprika.

Place onions in a 13- x 9- x 2-
inch baking dish. Cover and
bake at 350° for 20 minutes. Uncover and bake an additional 5
minutes. Yield: 6 servings.

Stuffed Vidalia Onions

Workers stop to pose for the camera during the harvesting of the onion crop on a farm near San Antonio, Texas, c.1920.

CRUNCHY ASPARAGUS WITH VIDALIA ONIONS

1 pound fresh asparagus spears
¼ cup vegetable oil
2 medium-size Vidalia onions, peeled
½ teaspoon salt
½ teaspoon coarsley ground black pepper
⅛ teaspoon dried whole oregano

Snap off tough ends of asparagus; remove scales from stalks with a knife or vegetable peeler. Cut asparagus diagonally into 1½-inch pieces; set aside.

Cut onions into thin slices. Heat ¼ cup oil in a wok or heavy skillet. Add asparagus pieces, onion slices, salt, pepper, and oregano; stir well. Cover and cook 8 minutes or until vegetables are crisp-tender. Drain before serving. Yield: 4 to 6 servings.

BAKED VIDALIA ONIONS

6 large Vidalia onions, peeled
¼ cup butter or margarine
Salt and white pepper to taste

Cut a ¼-inch slice from top and bottom of each peeled onion. Reserve slices for use in another recipe. Partially core each onion.

Place onions in a lightly greased 13- x 9- x 2-inch baking dish. Place 2 teaspoons butter in each onion. Cover dish tightly with aluminum foil, and bake at 400° for 1 hour. Uncover, and bake an additional 5 minutes or until tender. Sprinkle with salt and white pepper to taste. Yield: 6 servings.

BAKED VIDALIA ONIONS IN SHERRIED CREAM SAUCE

6 large Vidalia onions, peeled, sliced, and parboiled
¼ cup butter or margarine
¼ cup all-purpose flour
2 cups half-and-half
⅔ cup sherry
2 (2.5-ounce) jars sliced mushrooms, drained
¼ cup chopped pimiento
1 teaspoon salt
¼ teaspoon pepper
1½ cups (6 ounces) shredded sharp Cheddar cheese

Place onions in a 12- x 8- x 2-inch baking dish, and set aside.

Melt butter in a heavy saucepan over low heat; add flour, stirring until smooth. Cook 1 minute, stirring constantly. Gradually add half-and-half; cook over medium heat, stirring constantly, until thickened and bubbly. Stir in sherry, mushrooms, pimiento, salt, and pepper; pour sauce over onions.

Bake, uncovered, at 350° for 25 minutes. Sprinkle cheese over top of sauce; bake an additional 5 minutes or until cheese melts. Yield: 6 servings.

PARSNIPS

Creamed Parsnips (front) and Parsnip Fritters.

HOW TO PREPARE FRESH PARSNIPS

2 pounds parsnips
Salt to taste
1 teaspoon lemon juice

To Clean: Select parsnips as you would carrots: small to medium size, and firm. Avoid large ones, as they are probably woody at the center. Wash with brush and scrape, if desired. Parsnips may be shredded or sliced as indicated in recipe.

To Boil: Cut parsnips into ⅛-inch slices. Combine parsnips, salt, and lemon juice in a saucepan; add water to cover, and bring to a boil. Reduce heat; cover and simmer 10 minutes or until parsnips are tender. Drain. Yield: 6 to 8 servings.

Other Cooking Methods: Deep-fry; sauté; simmer; steam.

Serving Suggestions: Parsnips may be served with any of the following: Dill Sauce, Horseradish Sauce, Lemon-Butter Sauce, Mustard Dip Sauce, or any sour cream or white sauce.

"If parsnips are young, scrape and throw into cold water; if old, pare and cut in quarters. Put them into a saucepan of boiling water and boil until tender. . . . When done, lay on heated dish, heads all one way, cover with cream sauce or drawn butter, and serve."

Annie Dennis Cookbook, 1901

Bloomer girls turn their efforts to farming during World War I. The costume was named for Amelia Bloomer, 1800s crusader for temperance and women's lib.

PARSNIP PUREE

1½ pounds parsnips, scraped and cut into ¼-inch slices
½ cup butter or margarine
½ teaspoon dried whole thyme
½ teaspoon salt
Dash of white pepper
¾ cup dry white wine
¾ cup whipping cream

Sauté parsnips in butter 5 minutes; add thyme, salt, pepper, and wine, stirring well. Cover and simmer 15 minutes or until parsnips are tender. Combine parsnip mixture and whipping cream in container of an electric blender; process until pureed.

Return mixture to a medium saucepan; cook over low heat, stirring frequently, until thoroughly heated. Serve warm in bowls. Yield: 6 servings.

CREAMED PARSNIPS

2 tablespoons butter or margarine
2 tablespoons all-purpose flour
2 cups half-and-half
2 pounds parsnips, scraped, diagonally sliced, and boiled
1 teaspoon salt
½ teaspoon pepper

Melt butter in a heavy saucepan over low heat; add flour, stirring until smooth. Cook 1 minute, stirring constantly. Gradually add half-and-half; cook over medium heat, stirring constantly, until thickened and bubbly. Stir in parsnips, salt, and pepper; cook until thoroughly heated. Yield: about 8 servings.

PARSNIP FRITTERS

1 pound parsnips, scraped
1 teaspoon lemon juice
1¼ cups all-purpose flour
½ teaspoon sugar
¼ teaspoon baking powder
Dash of salt
¾ cup milk
1 egg, beaten
Vegetable oil

Soak parsnips in cold water 30 minutes. Drain; cut into 3-inch strips.

Combine parsnips, lemon juice, and a small amount of boiling salted water in a medium saucepan. Cover, and cook 10 minutes or until parsnips are tender. Drain well.

Combine flour, sugar, baking powder, and salt; stir well. Add milk and egg; beat until smooth.

Dip parsnip strips into batter; fry in deep hot oil (375°) until golden, turning once. Drain well on paper towels. Yield: 6 servings or 12 appetizer servings.

Serving Suggestion: Serve Parsnip Fritters with Mustard Dip Sauce.

BUTTERED PARSNIPS WITH PARSLEY

2 pounds parsnips, scraped and shredded
⅔ cup water
¼ cup butter or margarine, melted
1 teaspoon sugar
1 teaspoon salt
⅓ cup chopped fresh parsley

Place parsnips, water, butter, sugar, and salt in a small Dutch oven; bring to a boil. Reduce heat; cover and simmer 15 minutes, stirring occasionally. Toss with parsley before serving. Yield: 6 to 8 servings.

Fresh produce is displayed in this photograph taken in a Richmond, Virginia, market early this century.

BAKED PARSNIPS

1 pound parsnips, scraped
⅓ cup sugar
Salt to taste
Butter or margarine
1 tablespoon hot water
1 tablespoon whipping cream

Place parsnips in a medium saucepan; add water to cover. Bring to a boil; cover and cook 10 minutes or until tender. Drain parsnips, and place in a buttered 1½-quart baking dish. Sprinkle parsnips with sugar and salt; dot with butter.

Combine hot water and whipping cream. Pour over parsnips. Bake at 350° for 25 minutes or until lightly browned. Yield: 4 to 6 servings.

PARSNIP CAKES

1 pound parsnips, scraped and boiled
2 tablespoons butter or margarine, softened
2 tablespoons milk
½ teaspoon salt
⅛ teaspoon pepper
3 tablespoons flour
2 tablespoons bacon drippings

Mash parsnips; add butter, milk, salt, and pepper. Beat at medium speed of an electric mixer 2 minutes.

Shape into patties 2 inches in diameter and ½-inch thick; dredge patties in flour. Fry in hot drippings until golden brown, turning once. Drain well. Yield: 4 to 6 servings.

PEAS

HOW TO PREPARE FRESH GREEN PEAS

2 pounds fresh green peas
   (about 4 cups shelled)
2 teaspoons salt

To Shell: Fresh green peas or English peas should be shelled before cooking. Simply snap off the top of the pod, and pull the string down the side of the pod. Remove peas, and rinse in cold water; drain. (For sugar or edible-pod peas remove the tips and rinse in cold water.)

To Boil: Fill a large Dutch oven half full of water; add salt and bring to a rolling boil. Add shelled peas; bring back to a boil. Cook 6 minutes or until peas are tender. Drain well. Season and serve immediately. Yield: 4 servings.

Note: If green peas are to be served cold in salads, drop cooked peas immediately into cold water. Cool completely. Drain well.

Other Cooking Methods: Poêle; simmer; steam.

Serving Suggestions: Green peas may be served with butter and seasonings to taste or with any of the following: Drawn Butter, French Dressing, Lemon-Butter Sauce, Oil and Lemon Sauce, or any sour cream or white sauce.

Minted Green Peas with Onions: a lively springtime combination.

SOUTHERN-COOKED GREEN PEAS

3 cups shelled fresh
  green peas, cleaned
  (about 3 pounds
  unshelled)
1 cup water
¼ pound salt pork
½ teaspoon salt
2 tablespoons butter
  (optional)

Combine green peas, water, salt pork, and salt in a small Dutch oven. Bring to a boil; reduce heat. Cover and simmer 25 minutes or until peas are tender. Drain; add butter, if desired, and toss lightly. Yield: 6 servings.

MINTED GREEN PEAS WITH ONION

¼ cup plus 2 tablespoons
  butter or margarine
3 slices bacon
6 cups shelled fresh green
  peas, cleaned (about 6
  pounds unshelled)
4 dozen pearl onions, peeled
1 tablespoon chopped fresh
  mint
¾ cup boiling water
3 egg yolks, slightly beaten
1 cup whipping cream
1 tablespoon salt
1½ teaspoons pepper

Melt butter in a large Dutch oven; add bacon, and sauté until crisp. Remove bacon, and reserve for other uses.

Add peas, onions, mint, and boiling water to pan drippings. Cover and simmer 20 minutes or until peas are tender. Drain and set aside; keep warm.

Combine egg yolks, whipping cream, salt, and pepper; stir well. Pour sauce over peas and onions. Yield: 12 servings.

I hope that you will take the hint,
For love is warm as pepper—"Mint."

Affection expressed in a postcard, c.1890, is not without a touch of humor.

CREAMED GREEN PEAS AND POTATOES

2 cups shelled fresh green
  peas, cooked (about 2
  pounds unshelled)
6 small potatoes, peeled and
  cooked
¾ cup whipping cream
1 tablespoon all-purpose flour
1 teaspoon salt
Dash of red pepper

Combine peas, potatoes, and whipping cream in a medium saucepan; place over low heat. Combine flour and a small amount of water, stirring to make a smooth paste. Add flour mixture to peas and potatoes, stirring well. Cook over low heat until thickened. Stir in salt and pepper. Yield: 6 servings.

BUTTERED GREEN PEAS

1 medium onion, finely
  chopped
¼ cup butter or margarine
2 cups shelled fresh green
  peas, cleaned (about 2
  pounds unshelled)
½ head lettuce, shredded
½ cup chicken broth

Sauté onion in butter in a medium saucepan until tender. Add peas, lettuce, and chicken broth. Cover and simmer 15 minutes or until peas are tender. Yield: 4 servings.

BAKED GREEN PEAS

6 slices bacon, chopped
4 cups shelled fresh green peas, cooked (about 4 pounds unshelled)
1 cup whipping cream
1 teaspoon salt
⅛ teaspoon pepper
½ cup soft breadcrumbs
1 tablespoon melted butter or margarine
Pinch of salt and pepper
6 slices bacon, cooked and crumbled

Combine chopped bacon, peas, whipping cream, 1 teaspoon salt, and ⅛ teaspoon pepper; stir well. Spoon mixture into a greased 2-quart casserole.

Combine breadcrumbs, butter, and remaining salt and pepper; toss lightly. Sprinkle breadcrumbs evenly over peas. Bake at 350° for 20 minutes. Garnish with crumbled bacon. Yield: 8 servings.

Label designers sought to catch the buyer's eye, as in this late 1800s label for a can of peas. Peter Durand patented the tin-plated can in 1810.

GREEN PEAS AND DROP DUMPLINGS

2½ cups shelled fresh green peas, cleaned (about 2½ pounds unshelled)
1 cup water
1 tablespoon butter or margarine
¼ teaspoon salt
Dash of pepper
1 cup all-purpose flour
2 teaspoons baking powder
¼ teaspoon salt
2 eggs, beaten
3 tablespoons milk

Combine peas, water, butter, ¼ teaspoon salt, and pepper; bring to a boil. Reduce heat; cover and simmer 15 minutes. Set aside.

Combine flour, baking powder, and ¼ teaspoon salt, mixing well. Add eggs and milk, stirring with a fork until dry ingredients are moistened.

Return peas to a boil, and drop batter by tablespoonfuls into boiling peas. Cover immediately; reduce heat, and simmer 10 minutes. Yield: about 6 servings.

The last word on cooking green peas from *The Southern Gardener*, 1840: "The common method of cooking this delicious vegetable, by boiling in water, is nearly destructive to its flavour, at least so says a lady who has sent us the following method of preparing them. . . . 'Place in the bottom of your sauce-pan, or boiler, several of the outside leaves of lettuce; put your peas in the dish with two ounces of butter in proportion to half a peck of peas; cover the pan or boiler close, and place over the fire; in thirty minutes they are ready for the table. They can either be seasoned in the pan or taken out. Water extracts nearly all the delicious quality of the green pea, and is as fatal to their flavour as it is destructive to a mad dog.' "

HOW TO PREPARE FRESH BLACK-EYED OR FIELD PEAS

1½ pounds unshelled fresh
  black-eyed or field peas
  (about 3 cups shelled)
¼ pound salt pork
1 teaspoon salt

To Clean: Southern peas such as black-eyed peas (cowpeas) and field peas such as brown and cream crowder peas need only to be shelled and rinsed in cold water before cooking. (Dried peas should be soaked before cooking using the same procedure as for dried beans on page 15.)

To Simmer: Combine peas, salt pork, salt, and water to cover in a Dutch oven; bring to a boil. Reduce heat; cover and simmer 1 hour and 15 minutes or until peas are tender. Yield: 6 servings.

Other Cooking Methods: Poêle; steam.

Serving Suggestions: Cooked Southern peas, fresh or dried, may be served with any of the following: Basil Vinegar, Chive Vinegar, Fresh Tomato Sauce, Hot Pepper Sauce, or Mason County Relish.

Southern-Cooked Black-Eyed Peas (top right) and Hoppin' John

SOUTHERN-COOKED BLACK-EYED PEAS

About ¼ pound ham
  hocks
1 teaspoon lemon-pepper
  marinade
1 quart water
2 cups shelled fresh
  black-eyed peas, cleaned
  (about 1 pound
  unshelled)
Salt to taste

Wash ham hocks; place in a Dutch oven with lemon-pepper marinade and water. Bring to a boil; reduce heat and simmer, uncovered, 1 hour. Add peas; cover and cook over medium heat 1½ hours or until peas are tender. Add salt to taste before serving. Yield: 4 servings.

HOPPIN' JOHN

1 cup dried black-eyed peas
½ pound salt pork, cut into
  ½-inch cubes
1 quart water
½ cup chopped onion
½ hot red pepper, seeded and
  coarsely chopped
1 cup uncooked regular rice
1 teaspoon salt
⅛ teaspoon pepper

Sort and wash peas; place in a Dutch oven. Cover with water 2 inches above peas; let soak overnight. Drain well.

Combine peas, salt pork, water, onion, and red pepper in a Dutch oven; bring to a boil. Reduce heat; cover and simmer 1 hour. Add remaining ingredients; bring to a boil. Reduce heat; cover and simmer an additional 30 minutes or until peas are tender. Yield: 8 servings.

These directions for the Southern way to cook peas come from *Saga of Texas Cookery*: "Throw the shelled peas mercilessly into hot water, and boil them until they 'cave in.' When you see they are well subdued, take them out and fry them about ten minutes in gravy — plenty of gravy, good fat meat gravy, and try to induce the gravy to marry and become social with the peas. When you see that the union is complete, so that no man can put them asunder, and would not wish to if he could, put them in a dish and eat them all."

North Carolinian with basket of peas.

CREOLE BLACK-EYED PEAS

6 cups shelled fresh
 black-eyed peas, cleaned
 (about 3 pounds unshelled)
1 tablespoon salt, divided
1 tablespoon bacon drippings
1 cup chopped onion
1 cup chopped celery
1 cup chopped green pepper
2 hot red peppers, seeded and
 chopped
⅓ cup vegetable oil
2 (14½-ounce) cans whole
 tomatoes, undrained
4 cups sliced okra

Combine peas, 2 teaspoons salt, bacon drippings, and water to cover in a large Dutch oven; bring to a boil. Reduce heat; cover and simmer 45 minutes.

Sauté onion, celery, and peppers in oil until vegetables are tender; add to peas. Stir in tomatoes, okra, and remaining salt. Simmer, uncovered, 30 minutes or until peas are tender. Yield: 12 servings.

PASSION PEAS

1 large onion, chopped
½ medium-size green pepper,
 seeded and chopped
2 jalapeño peppers, seeded
 and finely chopped
2 stalks celery, chopped
½ cup catsup
1 tablespoon hot sauce
3 chicken-flavored bouillon
 cubes
1 tablespoon salt
1 teaspoon pepper
¼ teaspoon ground cinnamon
¼ teaspoon ground nutmeg
2 (16-ounce) cans black-eyed
 peas, undrained
1 (8-ounce) can stewed
 tomatoes, undrained and
 chopped
1 teaspoon garlic powder
½ cup bacon drippings
3 tablespoons all-purpose
 flour
Corn chips

Combine onion, peppers, celery, catsup, hot sauce, bouillon cubes, salt, pepper, cinnamon, and nutmeg in a large Dutch oven. Cook over medium heat 10 minutes; add peas, tomatoes, and garlic powder, stirring well. Cook over low heat 30 minutes, stirring occasionally.

Heat bacon drippings in a saucepan. Add flour; stir until smooth. Add mixture to peas; stir well. Cook 10 minutes, stirring frequently. Serve peas hot or cold with corn chips. Yield: 10 to 12 servings.

BLACK-EYED PEAS IN "POT LIKKER"

6 cups shelled fresh
 black-eyed peas, cleaned
 (about 3 pounds unshelled)
½ pound salt pork
2 teaspoons sugar
1½ teaspoons salt
6 cups water

Combine all ingredients in a large Dutch oven; bring to a boil. Reduce heat; cover and simmer 1 hour and 15 minutes or until peas are tender. Yield: 12 servings.

AUNT SIVIE'S GREEN CROWDER PEAS

About ¼ pound ham hocks
3 cups water
2 cups shelled fresh crowder
 peas, cleaned (about 1
 pound unshelled)
1 teaspoon salt

Wash ham hocks and place in a large Dutch oven. Add water, peas, and salt; bring to a boil. Reduce heat; cover and simmer 1 hour or until peas are tender. Yield: 8 servings.

Serving Suggestion: Aunt Sivie's Green Crowder Peas may be served with Hot Pepper Sauce.

BLACK-EYED PEAS WITH ONION

2 cups dried black-eyed
 peas
4 cups water
2 teaspoons salt
½ teaspoon pepper
¼ pound salt pork
1 medium onion, finely
 chopped

Sort and wash peas; place in a Dutch oven. Cover with water 2 inches above peas; let soak overnight. Drain well.

Combine peas, water, salt, pepper, and salt pork in a Dutch oven; bring to a boil. Reduce heat; cover and simmer 1½ hours or until peas are tender. Serve with chopped onion. Yield: 8 servings.

Athens, Texas, is known as the "Black-Eyed Pea Capital of the World." Black-eyed peas (or cowpeas) are not peas at all; they are black-pigmented lentils. Our custom of eating them on New Year's Day for luck goes far back to the Egyptian pharaohs.

PEPPERS

HOW TO PREPARE GREEN PEPPERS

6 medium-size green peppers
¼ cup butter or margarine
1 teaspoon salt
¼ teaspoon pepper

To Clean: Cut off tops of green peppers; discard tops. Remove stem, white membrane, and all seeds, as the seeds can be as hot as those of chile peppers. Wash and cut as directed in recipe.

To Parboil: Place whole peppers in a saucepan of boiling salted water; cook 5 minutes. Invert on rack to drain.

To Smother: Cut green peppers into 1-inch strips. Melt butter in a large skillet over low heat; add peppers, salt, and pepper. Cover and cook 15 minutes or until tender, turning once. Serve immediately. Yield: 4 servings.

Other Cooking Methods: Deep-fry; stuff and bake.

Serving Suggestions: Green peppers may be served with: Butter Sauce, Cheese Sauce, Dill Sauce, Fresh Tomato Sauce, Lemon-Butter Sauce, or any sour cream sauce. Peppers may also be sliced or chopped and served raw in salads.

Lithograph, appropriately called Vegetables, *by Grant Wood, 1938.*

Chili Stands, *a painting by Clara M. Cowsar, shows Mexican food vendors in San Antonio's Military Plaza, c.1882.*

STUFFED GREEN PEPPERS

4 ripe tomatoes, peeled and finely chopped
1 cup minced onion
1 cup chopped celery
1 cup uncooked regular rice
½ teaspoon salt
¼ teaspoon pepper
6 large green peppers, cleaned and parboiled
Butter or margarine

Combine first 6 ingredients; stir well. Stuff peppers with mixture; dot with butter. Place peppers in a lightly greased 5-quart casserole; cover and bake at 350° for 1 hour and 15 minutes. Yield: 6 servings.

Sharp, pungent chile peppers are as much a part of cooking in Texas as they are south of the border. Most famous is the tabasco, native to Mexico, grown commercially on Avery Island, Louisiana.

GREEN PEPPERS STUFFED WITH FRESH VEGETABLES

¼ cup chopped onion
2 tablespoons chopped celery leaves
1 tablespoon chopped fresh parsley
2 tablespoons butter or margarine
1 cup cooked green beans, cut into ½-inch pieces
1 cup whole kernel corn
1 medium tomato, peeled, seeded, and chopped
¼ teaspoon salt
¼ teaspoon dried whole marjoram
⅛ teaspoon dried whole basil
⅛ teaspoon dried whole dillweed
⅛ teaspoon coarsely ground pepper
4 medium-size green peppers, cleaned and parboiled
½ cup (2 ounces) shredded Cheddar cheese

Sauté onion, celery leaves, and parsley in butter in a large skillet until tender. Add next 8 ingredients; stir lightly.
Stuff mixture into green peppers. Place in a lightly greased shallow baking dish, and bake at 350° for 20 minutes. Top peppers with cheese. Bake an additional 5 minutes or until cheese melts. Yield: 4 servings.

CHILES RELLENOS WITH CHEESE

6 whole green chile peppers, cleaned and parboiled
2 cups (8 ounces) shredded Cheddar cheese
½ cup milk
½ cup all-purpose flour
2 eggs, separated
Vegetable oil
Salsa de Tomates

Stuff peppers with shredded cheese. Dip in milk, and dredge in flour. Set aside.
Beat egg whites (at room temperature) in a large mixing bowl until stiff peaks form. Beat egg yolks until thick and lemon colored; gently fold yolks into beaten egg whites.
Dip each pepper in egg mixture, and fry in deep hot oil (400°) for 2 to 3 minutes or until lightly browned, turning once. Drain well on paper towels. Serve with Salsa de Tomates. Yield: about 4 servings.
Note: For guests, you may want to serve a variety of additional sauces, such as Hot Pepper Sauce, Fresh Tomato Sauce, Cheese Sauce, or any sour cream sauce.

Salsa de Tomates:

1 medium onion, chopped
1 clove garlic, minced
2 tablespoons olive oil
1 (16-ounce) can stewed tomatoes, undrained
1 teaspoon chili powder
¼ teaspoon salt

Sauté onion and garlic in olive oil in a large skillet until tender. Stir in tomatoes, chili powder, and salt; simmer 30 minutes or until sauce is thickened. Yield: about 1½ cups.

Chiles Rellenos. Texans remember them made with fresh green chiles, roasted in the oven, steamed in a hot wet cloth, and then peeled. They believe they were better than today's canned ones.

Stuffed Banana Peppers will be a pleasant surprise.

GREEN PEPPER PIE

1 cup diced bacon
3 cups finely chopped green
   pepper
2 cups shredded onion
1 teaspoon sugar
½ teaspoon salt
¼ teaspoon pepper
1 baked 9-inch pastry shell
1⅓ cups commercial sour
   cream
Tomato wedges
3 slices bacon, cooked and
   crumbled

Cook diced bacon in a large skillet until crisp; drain well. Crumble and set aside. Drain off drippings, reserving 2 table-spoons in skillet.

Add green pepper and onion to skillet. Cover and cook over medium heat 15 minutes, stirring occasionally. Add sugar, salt, and pepper; mix well.

Spoon mixture into pastry shell; spread sour cream evenly over top. Garnish with tomato wedges and bacon. Bake at 350° for 30 minutes. Cut into wedges. Yield: 6 to 8 servings.

Samples of every pepper known (all capsicums) would probably fill a gymnasium. The green or bell pepper of the United States was cultivated in South America well before the time of Columbus, who carried the seeds on his trip back home to Spain. The red peppers of the temperate zone are used as table vegetables and, sometimes, as a medicine. Pimiento peppers serve as stuffing for olives and go into one of the South's favorite sandwich fillings, pimiento cheese. We dote, too, on stuffed peppers, and make a wonderful jelly from green or red-ripe sweet peppers, sometimes with some hot ones thrown in.

STUFFED BANANA PEPPERS

12 large sweet banana
   peppers
1 small tomato, finely
   chopped
½ cup finely chopped
   onion
¼ cup finely chopped
   sweet pickle
¼ cup finely chopped
   green pepper
2 small hot peppers,
   seeded and finely
   chopped
2 cups (8 ounces)
   shredded sharp Cheddar
   cheese
⅛ teaspoon salt
⅛ teaspoon pepper
12 slices bacon

Slit each banana pepper lengthwise, and carefully remove seeds. Wash and set aside.

Combine next 8 ingredients in a large bowl, mixing well.

Stuff each banana pepper with cheese mixture. Wrap a bacon slice around each stuffed pepper, securing well with a wooden pick.

Place peppers on a well-greased rack in broiler pan. Bake at 400° for 35 minutes or until bacon is crisp. Yield: 12 servings.

Serving Suggestions: Stuffed Banana Peppers may be served with Dill Sauce, Fresh Tomato Sauce, or any sour cream sauce.

POTATOES

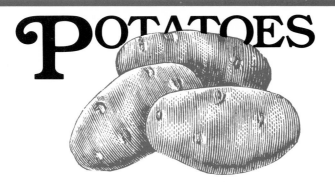

HOW TO PREPARE POTATOES

4 medium potatoes
Butter or margarine
Salt and pepper to taste

To Clean: Wash potatoes, and scrub thoroughly using a vegetable brush. Rinse with cold water, and drain. Bake or boil without peeling, as many of the nutrients are just under the skin. Small, whole new potatoes are at their best cooked in their pink jackets. If peeled, potatoes will darken quickly. Cook immediately or place them in lightly salted cold water to prevent darkening. For deep-fried potatoes, ice the water; drain and dry thoroughly before frying.

To Bake: Place potatoes on center rack of oven. Bake at 400° for 1 hour or until potatoes yield slightly to pressure.

Cut a slit in the top of each baked potato. Press sides to loosen inside of potato. Add butter and seasonings to taste. Yield: 4 servings.

Note: To yield a crispy potato skin, rub with shortening before baking. To keep potatoes hot until serving time, remove from oven, and roll up (jellyroll fashion) in a clean towel; put in a warm place.

To Boil: Combine potatoes and water to cover in a medium saucepan. Bring to a boil; reduce heat, and cook 25 minutes or until tender. Drain; peel, if desired. Add butter and seasonings to taste. Yield: 4 servings.

Other Cooking Methods: Fry; deep-fry.

Serving Suggestions: Baked or broiled potatoes may be served with any of the following: Cream Mint Spread, Cheese Sauce, Drawn Butter, any herb butter or spread, or any sour cream sauce.

An 1853 Nathaniel Currier lithograph in a series of American scenes.

QUICK-BAKED POTATOES

4 medium potatoes,
  cleaned
Butter or margarine
Salt and pepper to taste

Combine potatoes and water to cover in a medium saucepan; bring to a boil. Reduce heat, and cook 20 minutes. Drain.

Place potatoes on center rack of oven. Bake at 400° for 15 minutes or until potatoes yield slightly to pressure. Cut a slit in the top of each potato. Press sides to loosen inside of potato. Add butter and seasonings to taste. Yield: 4 servings.

Baked Potatoes, white and sweet: Of all the ways in which potatoes can be prepared, many prefer the simplicity of plain baked.

STUFFED BAKED POTATOES

4 medium potatoes, cleaned
  and baked
¼ cup butter or margarine
¾ cup whipping cream
2 eggs, separated
1 teaspoon salt
⅛ teaspoon pepper
Paprika

Cut potatoes in half lengthwise; carefully scoop out pulp, leaving a ⅛-inch shell. Spoon pulp into a mixing bowl. Add butter, whipping cream, egg yolks, salt, and pepper; beat until fluffy.

Beat egg whites (at room temperature) until stiff peaks form; fold into potato mixture. Stuff potato shells with potato mixture; sprinkle with paprika. Bake at 400° for 10 minutes. Yield: 8 servings.

BOILED POTATOES WITH JACKETS

4 medium potatoes, cleaned
1 teaspoon salt
Butter or margarine, melted
  (optional)
Salt to taste (optional)

Soak potatoes in cold water to cover for 1 hour; drain.

Cook potatoes in boiling water to cover 25 minutes. Add 1 teaspoon salt, and cook an additional 10 minutes or until tender. Drain well. Serve with melted butter and salt to taste, if desired. Yield: 4 servings.

Woman peeling potatoes on her neatly kept back porch.

BOILED POTATOES WITHOUT JACKETS

4 medium potatoes, cleaned
  and peeled
¼ cup whipping cream
2 tablespoons melted
  butter
1 teaspoon salt
⅛ teaspoon pepper

Place potatoes in a medium saucepan with water to cover. Bring to a boil; reduce heat, and cook 30 minutes or until potatoes are tender. Drain well; place in serving dish.

Combine whipping cream, butter, salt, and pepper. Pour mixture over potatoes. Serve immediately. Yield: 4 servings.

BOILED NEW POTATOES

1 pound new potatoes,
  cleaned
½ teaspoon salt
2 tablespoons butter or
  margarine, melted
¼ teaspoon white pepper

Combine potatoes, salt, and 1 inch water in a medium saucepan. Bring to a boil. Reduce heat; cover and simmer 20 minutes or until tender. Drain.

Pare a 1-inch strip around center of each potato. Combine butter and pepper. Add potatoes, and toss lightly to coat well. Serve immediately. Yield: 4 servings.

CREAMED POTATOES

4 medium potatoes, cleaned
  and peeled
1 teaspoon salt
¼ cup all-purpose flour
⅓ cup butter
3 tablespoons finely chopped
  onion
2 cups whipping cream

Cut potatoes into ⅛-inch-thick slices; place in a bowl of salted water, and soak 1 hour. Drain well.

Place one-fourth of the potatoes in a greased 2-quart casserole; top with one-fourth each of salt and flour. Dot with one-fourth of butter and onion. Repeat layers 3 more times.

Pour whipping cream over final layer. Cover and bake at 350° for 45 minutes; uncover and bake an additional 15 minutes or until lightly browned. Yield: 6 to 8 servings.

The Fine Arts Museums of San Francisco

ESCALLOPED POTATOES

6 medium potatoes, cleaned and peeled
¼ cup plus 1 tablespoon butter or margarine
¼ cup plus 1 tablespoon all-purpose flour
2 cups milk
1 teaspoon salt
½ teaspoon pepper
2 cups (8 ounces) shredded Swiss cheese
¼ cup chopped fresh parsley
¼ cup fine dry breadcrumbs
2 tablespoons butter or margarine

Cut potatoes into ⅛-inch-thick slices; place in a bowl of lightly salted water. Set aside.

Fill a medium Dutch oven one-fourth full of water; bring to a boil. Drain potatoes; add to boiling water. Cover and cook over medium heat 20 minutes or until tender; drain well and set aside.

Melt ¼ cup plus 1 tablespoon butter in a medium saucepan; add flour, stirring until smooth. Cook 1 minute, stirring constantly. Gradually add milk; cook over medium heat, stirring constantly, until thickened and bubbly. Add salt and pepper; stir well.

Alternate layers of white sauce, potatoes, cheese, and parsley in a greased shallow 2½-quart casserole, beginning and ending with sauce. Sprinkle top with breadcrumbs and dot with 2 tablespoons butter. Cover and bake at 350° for 15 minutes or until thoroughly heated. Yield: 8 servings.

Grant Wood's Dinner for Threshers, *painted c.1934.*

MASHED POTATOES

4 medium potatoes, cleaned
   and peeled
1 tablespoon plus 1½
   teaspoons butter or
   margarine
1 teaspoon salt
½ cup half-and-half

Cut potatoes into quarters.
Combine potatoes and boiling
water to cover in a large saucepan; cook 20 minutes or until
tender. Drain liquid, reserving
potatoes in saucepan; add butter and salt. Mash potatoes until
smooth. Add half-and-half; stir
well. Serve immediately. Yield: 4
servings.

MASHED POTATO PUFFS

½ cup all-purpose flour
1 teaspoon baking powder
½ teaspoon salt
2 medium potatoes, cooked,
   peeled, and mashed
   (about 1 cup)
1 egg, beaten
1 teaspoon chopped
   fresh parsley

Combine flour, baking powder, and salt. Add mashed potatoes, egg, and parsley, mixing
well. Drop mixture by teaspoon-
fuls into deep hot oil (375°); fry
until golden brown. Yield: about
2 dozen.

P are the potatoes; cover
them with cold water,
and boil gently until
done. Pour off the water, and
sprinkle salt over them;
using a spoon, take each potato and lay it into a clean,
warm cloth; twist this so as
to press all the moisture
from the vegetable, and ren-
der it quite round. . . . Potatoes dressed in this way are
mashed without the slight-
est trouble."

Practical Cooking and Dinner Giving, 1877

Vegetable Department.

"Potatoe Snow"

For this purpose use potatoes that
are white, mealy, and smooth.
Boil them very carefully and when
done, peel them, pour off the
water, and set them on a trivet
before the fire until they are
quite dry and powdery. Then rub
them through a coarse wire sieve
until the dish in which they
are to go to table is neatly heaped.
Do not disturb the potatoes before
they go to table, or the flakes will
fall and it will flatten. This
preparation looks well but many
thinks that it renders potatoes in-
sipid.

(N. B.) A very nice way of serving up
potatoes, (where cream is plenty,) is to
pour some hot cream over them, when
boiled & peeled, in which some butter has been

GREEK MASHED POTATO CAKES

5 to 6 medium potatoes,
   cooked, peeled, and mashed
   (about 2½ cups)
1 tablespoon butter or
   margarine, melted
1 egg, beaten
3 tablespoons Romano
   cheese
¼ teaspoon salt
⅛ teaspoon pepper
All-purpose flour
Vegetable oil

Combine potatoes, butter,
egg, cheese, salt, and pepper.
Using ¼ cup potato mixture per
patty, shape into 2½-inch patties, about ½-inch thick.

Heat ⅛ inch hot oil (375°) in a
skillet. Dredge each patty in
flour. Cook until golden brown,
turning once. Drain well. Yield:
4 servings.

OVEN-FRIED POTATOES

4 medium potatoes, cleaned
   and peeled
¾ cup vegetable oil
Salt to taste

Cut potatoes into ⅜-inch-
thick slices; cut each slice into
⅜-inch-thick strips.

Dip potato strips, several at a
time, into oil. Drain and place in
a single layer in a 15- x 10- x 1-
inch jellyroll pan. Bake, uncovered, at 425° for 50 minutes,
turning potato strips every 15
minutes. Drain on paper towels;
sprinkle with salt to taste. Yield:
8 to 10 servings.

*Potatoe Snow from
illustrated manuscript,
Recipes in the Culinary Art,
1852. Flaky and pretty,
but apparently almost too
delicate to be carried
to the table.*

BROWNED NEW POTATOES

2 tablespoons bacon
   drippings
1 pound new potatoes,
   cleaned, boiled, and peeled
1 tablespoon molasses

Heat bacon drippings in a
heavy skillet over medium heat;
add potatoes and cook, turning
frequently, 10 minutes or until
browned. Add molasses; stir to
coat potatoes. Reduce heat;
cook for 1 minute, stirring constantly. Yield: 4 servings.

FRIED NEW POTATOES

4 slices bacon
1 pound new potatoes,
   cleaned, boiled, and peeled
½ teaspoon salt
Dash of pepper

Cook bacon in a large skillet
until crisp; drain on paper
towels. Crumble and set aside,
reserving drippings in skillet.

Cook potatoes in drippings 10
minutes or until browned; turn
frequently. Drain. Place potatoes in serving dish; sprinkle
with salt, pepper, and crumbled
bacon. Yield: 4 servings.

PAN-FRIED POTATOES

4 medium potatoes, cleaned
   and peeled
¼ cup butter or margarine
1 teaspoon salt

Cut potatoes into ⅛-inch-
thick slices. Melt butter in a 10-
inch skillet over medium heat.
Add potatoes; cover and cook 10
minutes. Turn potatoes; cook,
uncovered, 10 minutes, turning
occasionally to brown. Drain
well. Sprinkle with salt. Yield: 6
to 8 servings.

Serving Suggestions: Pan-
Fried Potatoes may be served
with Dill Sauce, Horseradish
Sauce, Mustard Dip Sauce, or
any sour cream sauce.

The potato man in 1800s ad.

HASH BROWN POTATOES

1 tablespoon bacon drippings
2 cups cold, cooked, diced
   potatoes
½ teaspoon salt
Dash of pepper

Heat bacon drippings in a 10-
inch cast-iron skillet over medium heat. Add potatoes, salt,
and pepper; toss lightly to coat
well. Cook 4 minutes, stirring
constantly. Press potatoes to
one side of skillet forming an
omelet shape. Cook over medium heat 4 minutes or until
bottom of mixture is browned.

Transfer pan to oven, and
broil 4 inches from heat for 5
minutes or until top of potato
mixture is browned. Slide onto
a warm platter, and serve hot.
Yield: about 4 servings.

POTATO FRITTERS

6 medium potatoes,
  cleaned and peeled
¼ cup plus 1 tablespoon
  all-purpose flour
1 teaspoon salt
½ teaspoon white
  pepper
1 tablespoon vegetable oil
½ cup water
1 egg white
Additional vegetable oil

Cut potatoes into quarters; place in a medium saucepan with water to cover. Bring to a boil, and cook 10 minutes. Drain and cool; set aside.

Combine flour, salt, pepper, 1 tablespoon oil, and water, and set aside.

Beat egg white (at room temperature) until stiff but not dry; gently fold into flour mixture. Add potatoes, a few at a time, stirring gently to coat well. Drop each coated potato quarter into deep hot oil (375°). Fry until golden, turning once. Drain on paper towels. Serve immediately. Yield: 6 servings.

POTATO PANCAKES

3 medium potatoes, cleaned
  and peeled
1 tablespoon onion
1 egg, beaten
¼ cup all-purpose flour
1 teaspoon baking powder
½ teaspoon salt
⅛ teaspoon pepper
Vegetable oil

Cut potatoes into quarters; place in a medium saucepan with water to cover. Bring to a boil, and cook 10 minutes. Drain and cool.

Shred potatoes, and add remaining ingredients except oil, mixing well. Drop potato mixture by heaping tablespoonfuls into ⅛ inch hot oil (375°); press into 2½-inch rounds using the back of a fork. Fry until golden brown, turning once. Drain well. Yield: 6 servings.

SARATOGA POTATOES

4 medium potatoes, cleaned
  and peeled
Vegetable oil
Salt

Slice potatoes into very thin slices using a vegetable plane; place in ice water until slicing is completed. Drain potatoes well, and pat dry.

Carefully drop potato slices, a few at a time, into deep hot oil (375°). Fry 2 minutes or until golden brown. Drain well. Sprinkle with salt. Yield: 6 to 8 servings.

Note: Saratoga Potatoes may be served hot or cold.

Saratoga Potatoes will be instantly recognized as potato chips. They were a specialty with some cooks.

SWEET POTATOES

HOW TO PREPARE SWEET POTATOES

4 medium-size sweet potatoes
Butter or margarine

To Clean: Wash sweet potatoes in cold water; scrub vigorously using a vegetable brush. Rinse and drain. Sweet potatoes, like Irish potatoes, should be cooked whole without peeling when possible because most of the nutrients are next to the skin; they are also difficult to peel when raw. Sweet potatoes will darken rapidly after being pared raw but may be held briefly in lightly salted water until cooking time.

To Bake: Place potatoes on center rack in oven. Bake at 400° for 1 hour or until potatoes yield slightly to pressure.

Cut a slit in the top of each potato. Press sides to loosen inside of potato. Add butter to taste. Yield: 4 servings.

To Boil: Combine scrubbed whole potatoes and water to cover in a medium saucepan. Bring to a boil. Cover; reduce heat, and simmer 45 minutes or until tender. Drain and cool slightly. Peel skins from potatoes; discard skin. Cut potatoes into cubes or slices, or cut into cubes and mash. Add butter to taste. Yield: 4 servings.

Other Cooking Methods: Fry; deep-fry.

Serving Suggestions: Sweet potatoes may be served with Drawn Butter or with any sour cream sauce.

Sweet potatoes may be divided loosely into two types: the pale yellow sort with a drier flesh and the moist-meated deep orange kind. The sub-tropical yam was traditionally the natives' most important root crop and is considered one of nature's most complete foods. But the only form of wild yam known in the United States is not a food crop. The "yams" grown in Florida and Louisiana are sweet potatoes, but are called yams to differentiate them from the dryer, paler colored sweet potato.

Texans brag about sweet potato crops like this one.

FRIED SWEET POTATOES

4 medium-size sweet
  potatoes, cleaned and
  peeled
⅓ cup bacon drippings
Sugar

Slice potatoes into ¼-inch-
thick slices. Place in salted
water 30 minutes; drain.

Heat bacon drippings in a
large skillet; add potato slices.
Cook until tender and golden
brown, turning once. Drain on
paper towels. Sprinkle with
sugar. Yield: 6 servings.

FLUFFY SWEET POTATOES IN ORANGE SHELLS

8 small oranges
5 medium-size sweet
  potatoes, boiled, peeled, and
  mashed (about 4 cups)
½ cup milk
¼ cup firmly packed brown
  sugar
3 tablespoons honey
2 tablespoons butter or
  margarine, softened
Dash of salt
Dash of pepper
Dash of ground nutmeg
⅓ cup finely chopped pecans

Cut a thin slice from bottom
of each orange so that it will sit
flat. Cut a 1-inch slice from top
of oranges. Gently remove pulp,
leaving shells intact. Scallop
edges, and set aside.

Combine hot potatoes, milk,
sugar, honey, butter, salt, pepper, and nutmeg; mix well.
Spoon mixture into prepared orange cups; sprinkle with
pecans. Bake at 325° for 10 minutes. Yield: 8 servings.

Note: If desired, sweet potato
mixture can be piped into orange shells for a more festive ap-
pearance.

*Fluffy Sweet Potatoes in
Orange Shells and
Candied Sweet Potatoes.*

CANDIED SWEET POTATOES

6 medium-size sweet
  potatoes, cleaned and
  peeled
1 cup firmly packed brown
  sugar
2 teaspoons ground
  cinnamon
¼ cup plus 2 tablespoons
  butter or margarine, melted

Slice sweet potatoes lengthwise into ¼-inch-thick slices.

Arrange sweet potatoes in a
lightly greased 13- x 9- x 2-inch
baking dish. Sprinkle evenly
with sugar and cinnamon. Pour
melted butter over top.

Cover and bake at 350° for 30
minutes. Baste potatoes with
syrup formed in bottom of baking dish. Cover and continue
baking 25 minutes. Remove
cover, and bake 5 minutes or
until lightly browned. Yield: 8 to
10 servings.

*The Winter Garden district
of South Texas likes to
show off its pretty girls and
outsized vegetables.*

CANDIED SWEET POTATOES WITH LEMON SLICES

6 medium-size sweet
  potatoes, cleaned and
  boiled
1 cup sugar, divided
Ground cinnamon
1 large lemon, sliced
¾ cup water
2 tablespoons butter or
  margarine

Peel potatoes; slice lengthwise
into ¼-inch-thick slices.

Arrange half of sliced sweet
potatoes in a lightly greased 13-
x 9- x 2-inch baking dish. Sprinkle ½ cup sugar over sweet potatoes; sprinkle with cinnamon.
Arrange remaining potatoes
and lemon slices over top; sprinkle with remaining sugar and
cinnamon. Pour water over
sweet potatoes. Dot with butter.

Cover and bake at 350° for 30
minutes. Baste potatoes with
syrup formed in bottom of baking dish. Bake, uncovered, an
additional 10 minutes. Yield: 8
to 10 servings.

SWEET POTATO CROQUETTES

5 medium-size sweet
  potatoes, boiled, peeled, and
  mashed (about 4 cups)
½ cup milk
1 egg, beaten
2 tablespoons butter or
  margarine, melted
1 tablespoon sugar
1 teaspoon salt
2 eggs, well beaten
1½ cups cracker crumbs
Vegetable oil

Combine first 6 ingredients; beat at medium speed of an electric mixer until smooth. Shape potato mixture into croquettes using about ¼ cup mixture for each croquette.

Dip croquettes in egg, and roll in cracker crumbs. Fry in deep hot oil (375°) until golden brown. Drain; serve immediately. Yield: 1½ dozen.

SWEET POTATOES WITH MERINGUE

4 medium-size sweet
  potatoes, boiled, peeled, and
  mashed (about 3 cups)
3 eggs, separated
½ cup sugar, divided
3 tablespoons butter, melted
¼ cup milk
⅛ teaspoon salt
2 teaspoons sherry

Combine mashed potatoes, egg yolks, ¼ cup sugar, butter, milk, salt, and sherry; mix well. Spoon mixture into a greased 9-inch pieplate. Make a well in the center of mixture; smooth edges with a spatula.

Beat egg whites (at room temperature) until soft peaks form. Gradually add remaining sugar, 1 tablespoon at a time, beating until stiff peaks form.

Using a decorator bag and a medium-size tip, fill well with meringue, and make dollops around top of sweet potato mixture. Bake at 325° for 15 minutes or until the meringue is lightly browned. Yield: 10 to 12 servings.

SWEET POTATO PUDDING

5 eggs, beaten
1½ cups sugar
2 tablespoons butter or
  margarine, melted
3 cups grated raw sweet
  potatoes
2 cups milk
½ cup molasses
½ teaspoon salt
½ teaspoon ground cinnamon
½ teaspoon ground allspice
½ teaspoon ground nutmeg

Combine eggs, sugar, and butter in a large mixing bowl, beating well; stir in remaining ingredients. Pour into a 10-inch cast-iron skillet. Bake, uncovered, at 375° for 35 minutes or until top is browned; stir top crust under. Bake an additional 25 minutes or until a knife inserted in center comes out clean. Yield: 10 servings.

Note: Sweet Potato Pudding may be baked in a 1½-quart casserole, if desired.

VIRGINIA SWEET POTATO CASSEROLE

6 medium-size sweet
  potatoes, boiled, peeled, and
  mashed (about 4 cups)
½ cup butter or margarine,
  softened
¼ cup sugar
1 teaspoon ground
  cinnamon
1 teaspoon vanilla extract
1 (20-ounce) can crushed
  pineapple, undrained
1 cup golden raisins
16 large marshmallows

Combine mashed potatoes, butter, sugar, cinnamon, and vanilla; beat at medium speed of an electric mixer until smooth. Add crushed pineapple and raisins; stir well.

Spoon mixture into a well-greased 3-quart casserole. Bake at 350° for 15 minutes. Top with marshmallows. Bake an additional 10 minutes or until marshmallows are golden brown. Yield: 12 servings.

HOLIDAY SWEET POTATOES

4 medium-size sweet
  potatoes, boiled, peeled, and
  mashed (about 3 cups)
½ cup firmly packed brown
  sugar
½ cup butter or margarine,
  melted
1 tablespoon orange rind
1 teaspoon lemon rind
2 tablespoons plus 2½
  teaspoons orange juice
1 tablespoon lemon juice
½ teaspoon ground cinnamon
¼ teaspoon ground nutmeg
½ cup chopped pecans
¼ cup flaked coconut
1 tablespoon butter or
  margarine

Combine potatoes, sugar, ½ cup melted butter, rind, juice, cinnamon, and nutmeg; beat at medium speed of an electric mixer until smooth. Spoon mixture into a lightly greased 1-quart casserole.

Combine pecans and coconut; sprinkle over top of sweet potato mixture. Dot with 1 tablespoon butter. Bake at 350° for 20 minutes or until topping is lightly browned. Yield: 4 to 6 servings.

SWEET POTATO CASSEROLE

3 medium-size sweet
  potatoes, boiled, peeled, and
  mashed (about 2 cups)
1 cup sugar
2 eggs, slightly beaten
1 cup milk
½ cup butter or margarine,
  melted
½ teaspoon ground cinnamon
½ teaspoon ground nutmeg
1 teaspoon vanilla extract
½ cup chopped pecans

Combine potatoes, sugar, eggs, milk, butter, cinnamon, nutmeg, and vanilla; beat at medium speed of an electric mixer until smooth. Spoon mixture into a well-greased 1½-quart casserole. Sprinkle pecans over top. Bake, uncovered, at 350° for 1 hour. Yield: 8 servings.

One of the unpleasant side effects of the Revolutionary War was the deprivation of the colonists of imported foods blockaded out by the British. Tea, of course, was no longer consumed, and coffee was in short supply. Hunger was not unknown, and that is the theme of an interesting, if unsubstantiated, story: General Francis Marion (right), leader of a band of Southern irregulars, invited a British officer to dine under a flag of truce. The meal was sweet potatoes, the beverage vinegar and water. The Redcoat was so touched by the rebels' Spartan courage, the story goes, that he resigned his commission and sailed for home.

RUTABAGAS

HOW TO PREPARE RUTABAGAS

1 (2-pound) rutabaga
Butter or margarine
Salt and pepper to taste

To Clean: Rutabagas must be peeled before cooking. Scrub and peel thin layers of skin; cut as directed in recipe.

Pot o'Gold: A subtle blend of color and taste. Rutabaga, the turnip's yellow sister, is sometimes called the Swedish turnip.

To Boil: Cut rutabaga into ½-inch cubes. Place in a medium saucepan of boiling water. Cook, uncovered, 30 minutes or until tender. Season with butter and seasonings to taste. Yield: 4 servings.

Note: It is best to boil vegetables such as onions, cabbages, and rutabagas without a cover.

Other Cooking Methods: Bake; deep-fry; steam.

Serving Suggestions: Rutabagas may be served with any of the following: Drawn Butter, any herb butter or spread, or any sour cream or white sauce.

POT O' GOLD

1 (2-pound) rutabaga, peeled and cubed
3 large carrots, scraped and cut into ½-inch slices
1 tablespoon sugar
1 teaspoon salt
¼ cup butter or margarine

Fill a medium saucepan with ½-inch water. Add rutabaga, carrots, sugar, and salt; bring to a boil. Cook, uncovered, over low heat 35 minutes or until rutabaga is tender; drain. Add butter, and mash to desired consistency. Yield: 6 servings.

SOUTHERN-COOKED RUTABAGAS

1 (2-pound) rutabaga, peeled
  and cubed
3 cups water
¼ pound salt pork, rinsed
  and sliced
1 teaspoon sugar
½ teaspoon salt
⅛ teaspoon pepper
Additional pepper

Combine rutabaga, water, salt pork, sugar, and salt in a Dutch oven. Bring to a boil. Reduce heat; simmer, uncovered, 35 minutes or until rutabaga is tender. Drain. Remove salt pork; discard.

Add ⅛ teaspoon pepper to rutabaga; mash to desired consistency. Sprinkle with additional pepper. Yield: 4 to 6 servings.

RUTABAGA PUDDING

2 (2-pound) rutabagas,
  peeled and cubed (about
  6 cups)
1 cup whipping cream
4 eggs, beaten
½ cup butter or margarine,
  melted
1 small onion, finely
  chopped
3 tablespoons chopped
  fresh parsley
¾ teaspoon salt
Dash of pepper

Place rutabaga in a Dutch oven with water to cover. Bring water to boil. Reduce heat; simmer, uncovered, 40 minutes or until rutabaga is tender. Drain well; mash.

Combine rutabaga and remaining ingredients, mixing well. Spoon mixture into a lightly greased 2-quart casserole. Bake at 325° for 1 hour or until lightly browned. Yield: 8 to 10 servings.

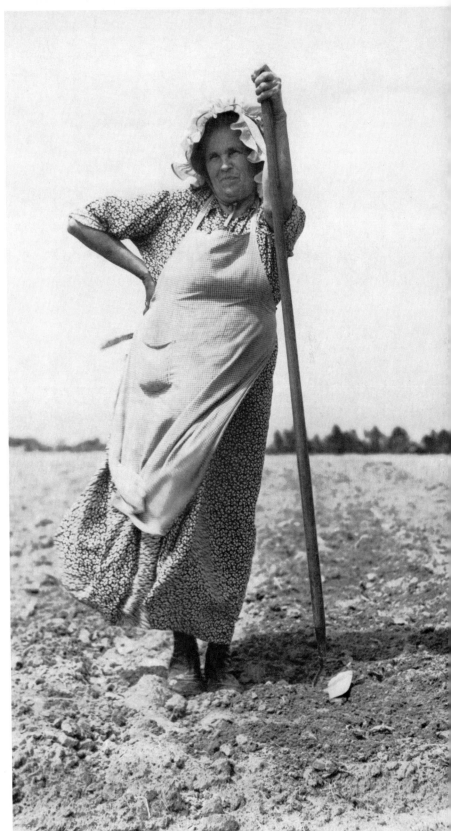

Wearing the standard dress for field work, a North Carolina woman leans briefly on her hoe for the photographer, c.1940.

Library of Congress

99

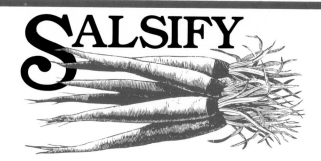

SALSIFY

HOW TO PREPARE FRESH SALSIFY

1 pound fresh salsify, scraped
¼ cup butter or margarine
Salt and pepper to taste

To Clean: Salsify is prepared exactly like carrots. Wash and scrub with a vegetable brush; peel with a vegetable peeler or scrape, if preferred. Cut into ⅛- to ¼-inch-thick slices. To prevent darkening, place sliced salsify in lightly acidulated water until cooking time.

To Boil: Cook salsify in a small amount of boiling salted water 10 minutes or until tender; drain well. Add butter and seasonings to taste. Yield: 4 servings.

Other Cooking Methods: Deep-fry; sauté.

Serving Suggestions: Salsify may be served with Almond Butter, Lemon-Butter Sauce, or any sour cream sauce.

Note: Canned salsify may be substituted in recipes calling for cooked fresh salsify.

SCALLOPED SALSIFY

14 saltine crackers, crushed
1 pound salsify, scraped, sliced, and cooked (about 2 cups)
½ teaspoon salt
¼ teaspoon paprika
1 tablespoon butter or margarine
¾ cup whipping cream
1 cup buttered breadcrumbs

Place cracker crumbs in bottom of a lightly greased 1-quart casserole. Add salsify; sprinkle with salt and paprika. Dot with butter. Pour cream over salsify; top with breadcrumbs. Bake, uncovered, at 400° for 30 minutes. Yield: 4 servings.

SALSIFY BISQUE

1 pound salsify, scraped, sliced, and boiled (about 2 cups)
¼ cup chopped celery
2 teaspoons chopped onion
1 teaspoon salt
⅛ teaspoon red pepper
3 cups half-and-half
2 egg yolks, beaten
Chopped fresh parsley

Combine half of salsify, celery, and onion in container of an electric blender; process until smooth. Repeat procedure with remaining vegetables.

Spoon salsify mixture into top of a double boiler. Add salt, pepper, and half-and-half; stir well. Place over simmering water; cook 6 minutes or until thoroughly heated. Remove top of double boiler from heat.

Gradually stir about one-fourth hot mixture into yolks; add to remaining hot mixture in top of double boiler, stirring well. Place over simmering water; cook, stirring constantly, until thickened. Garnish with parsley. Yield: 4 servings.

PICKLED SALSIFY

1 pound salsify, scraped and cut into 2-inch pieces
⅓ cup firmly packed brown sugar
3 tablespoons vinegar
1 tablespoon butter or margarine
½ teaspoon salt
¼ teaspoon pepper

Cook salsify in a small amount of salted boiling water 10 minutes or until tender; drain well. Set aside.

Combine sugar, vinegar, butter, salt, and pepper in a medium saucepan. Add salsify; cook over low heat 30 minutes or until thickened, stirring occasionally. Yield: 4 servings.

Salsify Bisque (rear) and Pickled Salsify. Oyster plant is salsify's alias.

SPINACH

HOW TO PREPARE FRESH SPINACH

3 pounds fresh spinach
1 tablespoon butter or margarine
1 teaspoon lemon juice
¼ teaspoon salt

To Clean: Discard any wilted or yellowed leaves and pulpy stems. Tear into bite-size pieces. Washing is the most important part of preparing spinach. Fill both bowls of a double sink (or sink and a large pan) with lukewarm water. Wash spinach by plunging up and down in one sink; lift spinach out of the water and into the other container of water. Repeat procedure, rinsing sink or pan between washings until no trace of sand remains in final rinse water.

Note: Spinach is not well washed unless lifted out of the water. Simply pulling the plug on the sink or pouring the water from the pan without first removing the spinach will not rinse away the sand.

To Steam: Place spinach in a steaming rack; cover and steam over boiling water 10 minutes. Place spinach in a warm serving dish. Combine butter, lemon juice, and salt; pour over spinach. Yield: 4 servings.

Other Cooking Methods: Boil; sauté.

Serving Suggestions: Spinach may be used raw in salads or cooked and served with any of the following: Basil Vinegar, Chive Blossom Vinegar, Chive Vinegar, Oil and Lemon Sauce, or Sweet-and-Sour Dressing.

Chilly shoppers examine produce at Center Market, Washington, D.C., c.1890.

SPINACH-EGG RAMEKINS

2 pounds fresh spinach, cleaned
2 tablespoons butter or margarine
2 teaspoons all-purpose flour
4 eggs
Cream sauce (recipe follows)
½ cup (2 ounces) shredded Cheddar cheese

Soak spinach in cold water to cover 1 hour. Drain. Place spinach in a large Dutch oven (do not add water); cover and cook over high heat 5 minutes or until tender. Drain spinach, reserving 2 tablespoons liquid. Chop spinach, and set aside.

Melt butter in a 10-inch skillet over low heat; add flour, stirring until smooth. Add spinach; cook 10 minutes over medium heat, stirring frequently. (If necessary, gradually add reserved liquid for desired consistency.) Spoon spinach mixture into 4 lightly greased 6-ounce custard cups. Set aside.

Fill a saucepan or skillet with 1½ inches salted water, and heat to boiling. When water boils, lower heat to simmer. Break eggs, one at a time, into a clean custard cup. Hold the lip of the cup close to water, and gently slip egg into the water. Simmer until eggs reach desired degree of doneness. (Do not allow water to boil.) Remove eggs with a slotted spoon, and drain well.

Place a poached egg on top of spinach in each custard cup. Cover each with cream sauce; top with cheese, and bake at 400° just until cheese melts. Serve hot. Yield: 4 servings.

Cream Sauce:

1 tablespoon plus 1½ teaspoons butter or margarine
1 tablespoon plus 1½ teaspoons all-purpose flour
½ cup milk
¼ teaspoon salt
⅛ teaspoon pepper

Melt butter in a heavy saucepan over low heat; add flour, stirring until smooth. Cook 1 minute, stirring constantly. Gradually add milk; cook over medium heat, stirring constantly, until thickened and bubbly. Stir in salt and pepper. Yield: about ½ cup.

SAUTÉED SPINACH SPECIAL

3 pounds fresh spinach, cleaned, cooked, and chopped
2 tablespoons olive oil
1 small onion, finely chopped
1 small clove garlic, minced
2 tablespoons vinegar
1 tablespoon bacon drippings
Pinch of red pepper
4 slices bacon, cooked and crumbled

Sauté spinach in olive oil for 5 minutes, stirring frequently. Remove from heat; set aside and keep warm.

Combine onion, garlic, vinegar, bacon drippings, and pepper in a small saucepan. Cook over medium heat 5 minutes. Remove from heat, and pour over spinach. Sprinkle bacon over top. Yield: 4 servings.

SPINACH AU GRATIN

3 pounds fresh spinach, cleaned and cooked
¼ cup plus 2 tablespoons grated Parmesan cheese
¼ cup plus 2 tablespoons finely chopped onion
¼ cup plus 2 tablespoons whipping cream
¼ cup butter or margarine, melted
½ teaspoon salt
⅛ teaspoon pepper
½ cup buttered breadcrumbs

Combine spinach, cheese, onion, whipping cream, butter, salt, and pepper; stir well. Spoon into a 1-quart casserole. Top with breadcrumbs. Bake at 450° for 10 minutes or until browned. Yield: 4 servings.

CRYSTAL CITY, TEX.

POPEYE ERECTED MARCH 26, 1937 COURTESY E.C. SEGAR

BOILED SPINACH

3 pounds fresh spinach, cleaned
½ teaspoon salt
¼ teaspoon pepper
1 tablespoon minced onion
1½ teaspoons butter or margarine
2 tablespoons soft breadcrumbs
2 tablespoons whipping cream
Salt and pepper to taste
1 hard-cooked egg, finely chopped

Place spinach in a large Dutch oven (do not add water); cover and cook over high heat 8 to 10 minutes. Drain spinach well. Add ½ teaspoon salt and ¼ teaspoon pepper, mixing well. Chop spinach, and set aside.

Sauté onion in butter until tender. Add chopped spinach, and sauté 5 minutes. Stir in 2 tablespoons breadcrumbs, whipping cream, and salt and pepper to taste.

Transfer spinach to a warm serving dish, and garnish with chopped egg. Yield: 4 servings.

The Menger Hotel, San Antonio, charged $2.00 per week in the early 1900s.

SPINACH TIMBALES

3 pounds fresh spinach, cleaned
¼ cup water
3 eggs, separated
1 tablespoon grated Parmesan cheese (optional)
½ teaspoon salt
¼ teaspoon sugar
¼ teaspoon ground nutmeg
⅛ teaspoon white pepper
1 cup whipping cream, divided
1 tablespoon butter or margarine
1 tablespoon all-purpose flour
¼ cup milk
¼ teaspoon salt
Dash of pepper
1 hard-cooked egg

Combine spinach and water in a Dutch oven. Bring to a boil; cover. Reduce heat; simmer 10 minutes. Drain well; chop.

Combine chopped spinach, egg yolks, cheese, if desired, ½ teaspoon salt, sugar, nutmeg, and white pepper in a medium saucepan. Cook over low heat 5 minutes, stirring constantly. Stir in ¾ cup whipping cream; cook 2 minutes, stirring constantly. Remove from heat.

Beat egg whites (at room temperature) until stiff peaks form; gently fold into spinach. Spoon into 4 lightly greased 6-ounce custard cups. Place cups in a pan with 1 inch hot water. Bake at 325° for 30 minutes or until a knife inserted in center comes out clean.

Melt butter in a heavy saucepan over low heat; add flour, stirring until smooth. Cook 1 minute, stirring constantly. Gradually add remaining ¼ cup whipping cream and milk; cook over medium heat, stirring constantly, until thickened and bubbly. Stir in ¼ teaspoon salt and pepper.

Separate hard-cooked egg. Chop the white; stir into sauce. Grate yolk, and set aside.

Loosen edges of timbales with a knife. Invert custard cups onto serving plate, and turn out. Spoon sauce evenly over timbales; top with grated egg yolk. Yield: 4 servings.

SPINACH WITH STUFFED EGGS

2 pounds fresh spinach, cleaned and cooked
1 tablespoon butter or margarine
⅛ teaspoon pepper
Salt to taste
2 hard-cooked eggs
2 tablespoons whipping cream
⅛ teaspoon curry powder
⅛ teaspoon paprika
¼ cup finely chopped cooked ham

Combine spinach, butter, pepper, and salt to taste, stirring well. Place spinach in a warm serving bowl; set aside, and keep warm.

Slice eggs in half lengthwise, and carefully remove yolks. Mash yolks; add whipping cream, curry powder, and paprika, mixing well. Stir in chopped ham. Stuff egg whites with yolk mixture; place stuffed eggs on cooked spinach. Yield: 4 servings.

Menger Hotel Spinach Loaf (front) and Spinach with Stuffed Eggs.

MENGER HOTEL SPINACH LOAF

4 cups finely chopped fresh spinach, cleaned (about 2½ pounds)
2 cups fine dry breadcrumbs
1 cup finely chopped onion
6 eggs, separated
½ cup butter or margarine, melted
1 teaspoon salt
½ teaspoon pepper
Lemon slices
Fresh spinach leaves

Combine chopped spinach, breadcrumbs, and onion, and set aside.

Beat egg yolks until thick and lemon colored. Add butter, salt, and pepper. Add spinach mixture; mix well. Set aside.

Beat egg whites (at room temperature) until stiff but not dry. Gradually add spinach mixture to egg whites; fold gently until well blended. Spoon into a lightly greased 8½- x 4½- x 3-inch loafpan.

Place loafpan into a 12- x 8- x 2-inch baking dish; pour hot water into dish to a depth of 1 inch. Bake at 350° for 50 minutes or until wooden pick inserted in center comes out clean. Invert spinach loaf onto a serving platter, and garnish with lemon slices and fresh spinach leaves. Yield: 1 loaf.

SQUASH

HOW TO PREPARE FRESH SUMMER SQUASH

2 pounds fresh summer squash (yellow, pattypan, or zucchini)

To Clean: The family of tender-skinned summer squash need only to be washed thoroughly in warm water, and the stem ends trimmed for cooking. Peeling is needed only if the squash is over-mature and tough. Summer squash may be prepared whole, cut in halves or slices, or cut in chunks and mashed, as indicated in the recipe directions.

To Boil: Place squash, either whole or cut into slices, in boiling salted water to cover. Cook 10 minutes or until tender. (Slices will cook in about 6 minutes.) Drain. Squash may be served whole or mashed. Yield: 4 servings.

Other Cooking Methods: Bake; fry; poêle; sauté; steam.

Serving Suggestions: Summer squash may be served with butter and seasonings to taste or with any of the following: Cheese Sauce, any herb butter or spread, or any white sauce.

1893 seed catalogue offers a wonderful world of squash.

SQUASH CAKES

1 pound yellow squash,
  cleaned and sliced
1 small onion, chopped
1 egg, beaten
¾ teaspoon salt
Dash of pepper
½ cup all-purpose flour
1 teaspoon baking powder
Vegetable oil

Combine squash and onion in a medium saucepan with boiling salted water to cover. Cook 10 minutes or until squash is tender; drain well. Mash squash and onion; drain once again. Stir in egg, salt, and pepper.

Sift flour and baking powder together. Add to squash mixture; mix well.

Drop mixture by tablespoonfuls into a small amount of hot oil (375°); brown on both sides. Drain well on paper towels. Yield: about 1½ dozen.

Serving Suggestions: Squash Cakes may be served with Horseradish Sauce or Mustard Dip Sauce.

CRUNCHY SQUASH CASSEROLE

1½ pounds yellow squash,
  cleaned, boiled, and
  mashed
1 small onion, finely
  chopped
1 tablespoon chopped fresh
  parsley
1 egg, beaten
¼ cup milk
½ cup small curd cottage
  cheese
1 teaspoon sugar
½ teaspoon salt
¼ teaspoon pepper
¼ cup finely chopped
  pecans

Combine mashed squash, onion, parsley, egg, milk, cottage cheese, sugar, salt, and pepper; mix well, and spoon into a lightly greased 1½-quart casserole. Sprinkle pecans over squash mixture. Bake, uncovered, at 350° for 50 to 55 minutes. Yield: 6 servings.

Pen and ink rendition of The Smith House, Dahlonega, Georgia.

SMITH HOUSE SQUASH CASSEROLE

¼ cup mayonnaise
¼ cup chopped onion
½ cup cracker crumbs,
  divided
1 egg, beaten
1 teaspoon sugar
¼ teaspoon salt
⅛ teaspoon pepper
1 pound yellow squash,
  cleaned, boiled, and mashed
¼ cup (1 ounce) shredded
  Cheddar cheese

Combine mayonnaise, onion, ¼ cup cracker crumbs, egg, sugar, salt, and pepper. Add mashed squash; mix well. Pour squash mixture into a lightly greased 1-quart casserole.

Sprinkle remaining cracker crumbs over squash mixture. Bake, uncovered, at 350° for 25 to 30 minutes; sprinkle cheese on top. Bake an additional 5 minutes or until cheese melts. Yield: 4 servings.

SAVORY SOUTHERN SQUASH

2 pounds yellow squash,
  cleaned and sliced
1 large onion, chopped
1 teaspoon salt
¼ teaspoon pepper
¼ cup bacon drippings

Combine squash and onion in a medium saucepan with boiling salted water to cover. Cook 10 minutes or until squash is tender; drain well.

Mash squash and onion; drain once again. Add salt and pepper; stir well.

Heat bacon drippings in a large skillet. Add mashed squash mixture. Cook over medium heat, stirring occasionally, 20 minutes or until mixture is browned. Yield: 2 to 4 servings.

FRIED PUMPKIN OR SQUASH BLOSSOMS

Gather blossoms while still in large bud, just ready to open. Wash carefully and press together flat. Dip in eggs, then in cornmeal or cracker crumbs. Add salt and pepper to taste; fry in hot shortening until brown. Serve as vegetable fritter. (From *Idle Hens Don't Lay*)

Note: For 12 blossoms, use 2 beaten eggs, 1 cup cornmeal, and ¼ teaspoon salt.

STUFFED CROOKNECK SQUASH

6 small yellow squash, cleaned
1 medium onion, chopped
2 tablespoons bacon drippings
1 tablespoon whipping cream
Dash of salt
⅛ teaspoon pepper
1 tablespoon Worcestershire sauce
¾ cup soft breadcrumbs
1 cup (4 ounces) shredded sharp Cheddar cheese
1 tablespoon butter or margarine, melted
Paprika

Place whole squash in a medium saucepan with boiling salted water to cover. Cook 10 minutes or until squash is tender. Drain well; cool slightly.

Cut a lengthwise slice from the top of each squash; remove and reserve pulp, leaving a firm shell. Mash pulp, and set aside.

Sauté onion in drippings over medium heat until tender. Remove from heat; add whipping cream, salt, pepper, Worcestershire sauce, and reserved squash pulp, stirring well.

Place squash shells in a lightly greased 13- x 9- x 2-inch baking dish. Spoon squash mixture into shells. Bake, uncovered, at 400° for 10 minutes. Combine breadcrumbs, cheese, and melted butter; stir well. Spoon cheese mixture evenly over each squash. Return to oven, and continue baking 5 minutes or until cheese melts. Sprinkle with paprika. Yield: 6 servings.

Zucchini Stuffed with Tomatoes (page 110) and Stuffed Crookneck Squash. All soft-skinned summer squash take well to various stuffings.

SQUASH DRUMSTICKS

4 small yellow squash, cleaned
1 small onion, quartered
½ cup cracker crumbs
½ teaspoon salt
¼ teaspoon pepper
¼ teaspoon paprika
2 eggs
2 tablespoons milk
Vegetable oil

Combine whole squash and onion in a medium saucepan with boiling salted water to cover. Cook 10 minutes or until squash is tender; drain well. Set squash aside. Discard onion.

Combine cracker crumbs, salt, pepper, and paprika; stir well. Combine eggs and milk, beating well. Dip each whole squash in egg mixture; dredge in cracker crumb mixture. Deep-fry in hot oil (375°) until golden brown. Drain on paper towels; serve immediately. Yield: 4 servings.

Serving Suggestions: Squash Drumsticks may be served with Dill Sauce, Horseradish Sauce, Mustard Dip Sauce, or any sour cream sauce.

PATTYPAN SQUASH CASSEROLE

2 pounds pattypan squash, cleaned
2 tablespoons butter or margarine
2 tablespoons chopped onion
2 tablespoons all-purpose flour
1 teaspoon salt
¼ teaspoon pepper
1 cup milk
1 cup soft breadcrumbs
2 tablespoons butter or margarine, melted

Cook squash, covered, in boiling salted water 20 minutes or until tender. Drain and mash. Drain again, if necessary.

Combine squash, 2 tablespoons butter, onion, flour, salt, pepper, and milk; stir well. Pour mixture into a lightly greased 1-quart casserole.

Combine breadcrumbs and melted butter; spoon over squash mixture. Bake, uncovered, at 350° for 30 minutes or until lightly browned. Yield: 4 to 6 servings.

A generous straw hat completes the gardening costume for the day, c.1917.

Brown Brothers

BAKED ZUCCHINI AND TOMATOES

2 medium zucchini, cleaned
Salt and pepper
¼ cup butter or margarine
3 medium tomatoes, peeled
   and sliced
1 medium onion, sliced
Butter or margarine
1 cup buttery cracker crumbs

Cut zucchini into ¼-inch-thick slices. Place zucchini in a 12- x 8- x 2-inch baking dish. Sprinkle with salt and pepper.

Layer half each of tomato and onion over zucchini; sprinkle each layer with salt and pepper. Dot each layer with butter. Repeat procedure, using remaining vegetables.

Sprinkle cracker crumbs over casserole. Bake at 350° for 40 minutes or until vegetables are tender. Yield: 8 servings.

ZUCCHINI STUFFED WITH TOMATOES

3 medium zucchini, cleaned
Salt and pepper
2 tablespoons butter or
   margarine
1 cup seasoned croutons
1½ cups finely chopped
   tomatoes
1 cup (4 ounces) shredded
   Cheddar cheese

Place whole zucchini in a medium saucepan with boiling salted water. Cook 10 minutes or until tender. Drain well.

Cut zucchini in half lengthwise; remove and reserve pulp for other uses, leaving a firm shell. Sprinkle each shell cavity with salt and pepper; set aside.

Melt butter in a medium saucepan. Add croutons, and toss gently. Combine buttered croutons with tomatoes. Mix well. Place zucchini shells in a lightly greased shallow baking dish; spoon tomato mixture into shells. Cover and bake at 450° for 20 minutes. Sprinkle with cheese; bake, uncovered, an additional 5 minutes or until cheese melts. Yield: 6 servings.

BUTTERED ZUCCHINI

1½ pounds zucchini,
   cleaned
3 tablespoons butter or
   margarine, melted
¼ teaspoon onion juice
Paprika

Cut zucchini into ¼-inch-thick slices. Place in a medium saucepan with boiling salted water to cover. Cook 10 minutes or until zucchini is tender. Drain well.

Transfer zucchini to a serving bowl. Combine butter and onion juice; pour evenly over zucchini. Sprinkle with paprika. Serve immediately. Yield: 4 to 6 servings.

STUFFED ZUCCHINI

6 medium zucchini,
   cleaned
2 cups buttery cracker
   crumbs
1 small onion, chopped
½ cup grated Parmesan
   cheese
3 tablespoons chopped
   fresh parsley
2 tablespoons butter or
   margarine, melted
1 teaspoon salt
⅛ teaspoon pepper
2 eggs, beaten
Additional grated
   Parmesan cheese

Place whole zucchini in a medium saucepan with boiling salted water. Cook 10 minutes or until tender. Drain.

Cut zucchini in half lengthwise. Scoop out pulp, leaving firm shells; chop pulp.

Combine chopped pulp, cracker crumbs, onion, ½ cup cheese, parsley, butter, salt, pepper, and eggs; mix well.

Place zucchini shells in a lightly greased 15- x 10- x 1-inch jellyroll pan. Spoon zucchini mixture into shells; sprinkle with additional Parmesan cheese. Bake at 350° for 30 minutes or until stuffing is lightly browned. Serve immediately. Yield: 12 servings.

Would you buy a can of Red Delaware tomatoes with such a label? Given the chance, we might today.

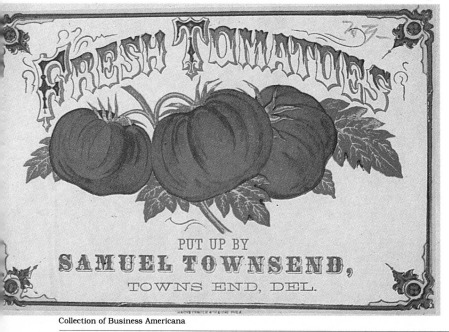

Creole Stuffed Chayote Squash. Some call chayote "mirliton."

SPECIAL STUFFED CHAYOTE SQUASH

3 medium-size chayote
   squash
1 medium onion, finely
   chopped
1 clove garlic, minced
1 tablespoon butter or
   margarine
1 medium tomato, peeled and
   chopped
2 tablespoons chopped fresh
   parsley
1 bay leaf, crushed
¼ teaspoon dried whole
   thyme
½ teaspoon salt
⅛ teaspoon pepper
¾ cup soft breadcrumbs
2 tablespoons butter or
   margarine
½ cup cooked, peeled,
   deveined shrimp, halved
½ cup buttered breadcrumbs

Wash squash thoroughly. Place in a medium saucepan with boiling salted water to cover. Cook 25 minutes or until tender. Drain and cool slightly.

Remove and discard squash seeds. Scoop out pulp, leaving a ¼-inch shell; mash pulp. Set aside squash shells and pulp.

Sauté onion and garlic in 1 tablespoon butter until tender. Stir in tomato, parsley, bay leaf, thyme, salt, and pepper, mixing well. Set aside.

Sauté reserved squash pulp and soft breadcrumbs in 2 tablespoons butter for 5 minutes. Stir in shrimp and reserved onion mixture. Spoon into squash shells. Sprinkle with buttered breadcrumbs.

Place stuffed squash in a shallow baking dish. Bake at 375° for 30 minutes or until browned. Yield: 6 servings.

CREOLE STUFFED CHAYOTE SQUASH

4 medium-size chayote
   squash
⅔ cup chopped green onion
⅓ cup chopped onion
¼ cup chopped fresh parsley
3 cloves garlic, minced
⅓ cup bacon drippings
1 cup chopped cooked ham
¾ cup soft breadcrumbs,
   divided
½ teaspoon salt
½ teaspoon pepper
Dash of hot sauce
1 egg, beaten

Wash squash thoroughly. Place in a medium saucepan with boiling salted water to cover. Cook 25 minutes or until tender. Drain and cool slightly.

Remove and discard squash seeds. Scoop out pulp, leaving a ¼-inch shell; chop pulp. Set aside shells and pulp.

Sauté onion, parsley, and garlic in bacon drippings until tender. Add ham; cook over medium heat 5 minutes, stirring occasionally. Add squash pulp, ½ cup breadcrumbs, salt, pepper, and hot sauce; cook 10 minutes. Remove from heat, and stir in egg.

Spoon stuffing mixture into squash shells. Place stuffed squash in a shallow baking dish; sprinkle with remaining breadcrumbs. Bake at 375° for 15 minutes or until breadcrumbs are lightly toasted. Yield: 8 servings.

CHAYOTE SQUASH, MISSISSIPPI STYLE

2 medium-size chayote
  squash
2 pounds medium shrimp,
  peeled, deveined, and
  cooked
2 tablespoons lemon juice,
  divided
½ cup chopped onion
½ cup chopped celery
½ cup chopped green
  pepper
¼ cup butter or margarine
1 (14½-ounce) can whole
  tomatoes, drained and
  chopped
2 bay leaves
2 teaspoons Worcestershire
  sauce
½ teaspoon hot sauce
¼ teaspoon dried whole
  oregano
⅛ teaspoon garlic powder
½ teaspoon salt
Dash of pepper
1 cup buttered breadcrumbs

Wash squash thoroughly. Place in a medium saucepan with boiling salted water to cover. Cook 25 minutes or until tender. Drain and cool slightly. Peel squash; remove seeds, and cube pulp. Set aside.

Combine shrimp and 1 tablespoon lemon juice. Let stand 10 minutes or until lemon juice is absorbed.

Sauté onion, celery, and green pepper in butter until tender. Stir in tomatoes, cubed squash, bay leaves, Worcestershire sauce, hot sauce, oregano, garlic powder, salt, and pepper. Cover and simmer 10 minutes. Remove bay leaves, and discard. Stir in shrimp and remaining lemon juice.

Spoon mixture into a lightly greased 2-quart casserole. Top with breadcrumbs. Bake at 350° for 20 minutes or until browned. Yield: 4 to 6 servings.

A New Orleans woman beams with pride as she holds up her prize cushaw squash.

WINTER SQUASH

HOW TO PREPARE WINTER SQUASH

2 medium winter squash
  (acorn, butternut, or
  hubbard)
¼ cup firmly packed brown
  sugar
2 tablespoons butter or
  margarine, softened

To Clean: Wash squash thoroughly in cold water. Cut in half and remove seeds and fiber from center of squash. Winter squash may be baked in halves or pieces without peeling or may be peeled and cut into chunks for mashing.

To Steam: Peel squash and cut into 1½-inch chunks. Arrange on steaming rack. Place over boiling water; cover and steam 15 minutes or until squash is tender.

Remove from heat, and sprinkle with brown sugar. Steam an additional 5 minutes. Transfer squash to a serving dish; dot with butter, and toss lightly to coat squash well. Yield: 6 to 8 servings.

Other Cooking Methods: Bake.

Pictured on the right is the original root cellar of Shirley Plantation with the manor house in the background. Located on the James River in Virginia, Shirley, like other colonial plantations, supported so many families that every pound of food grown that could be wintered over was beyond price. Root cellars were dug deep into the earth below frostline; vegetables thus stored were kept cool but in no danger of freezing. This repository held turnips, potatoes, both Irish and sweet, winter squash, carrots, parsnips, salsify, onions . . . and cabbage. Certainly no root, cabbage is nevertheless a good keeper, stored head down. Turnips and potatoes can be stored unharvested by banking the rows with earth.

Both the prize squash and its admirer seem larger than life, pictured at a local agricultural fair, c.1910.

Brown Brothers

BAKED ACORN SQUASH

2 large acorn squash, cleaned
¼ cup butter or margarine, melted
⅓ cup orange juice
½ cup firmly packed brown sugar
Orange slices (optional)

Place halves of squash, cut side down, in a shallow baking dish. Add 1 inch of water. Bake, uncovered, at 400° for 30 minutes or until tender.

Remove squash from baking dish, and cut into quarters. Place in a 13- x 9- x 2-inch baking dish.

Combine butter and orange juice; pour over squash. Sprinkle sugar over squash. Return to oven; bake 10 minutes. Garnish with orange slices, if desired. Yield: 8 servings.

WINTER SQUASH PUDDING

2 medium acorn squash, peeled, steamed, and mashed
1 cup sugar
2 tablespoons all-purpose flour
2 tablespoons butter or margarine, melted
1 tablespoon grated lemon rind
1 teaspoon salt
1 teaspoon ground cinnamon
1 cup milk
3 eggs, beaten
½ cup chopped pecans

Combine mashed squash, sugar, flour, butter, lemon rind, salt, and cinnamon in a large mixing bowl. Stir in milk and eggs, beating well.

Pour mixture into a lightly greased 2-quart baking dish. Sprinkle with pecans. Bake, uncovered, at 325° for 45 minutes or until set. Yield: 8 servings.

ORANGE-GLAZED ACORN SQUASH

1 large acorn squash
⅓ cup orange juice
¼ cup butter or margarine
½ cup firmly packed brown sugar
¼ cup corn syrup
2 teaspoons grated lemon rind
⅛ teaspoon salt

Wash squash thoroughly in cold water. Cut squash into ¾-inch slices to form rings, and remove seeds. Place squash rings in a lightly-greased 13- x 9- x 2-inch baking dish. Pour orange juice over squash rings. Cover with aluminum foil and bake at 350° for 40 minutes.

Melt butter in a small saucepan; add brown sugar, corn syrup, lemon rind, and salt, mixing well. Bring mixture to a boil; reduce heat, and cook 5 minutes, stirring constantly. Immediately spoon mixture over squash rings. Return to oven, and bake, uncovered, 20 minutes or until squash is tender. Yield: 8 servings.

SMITH HOUSE GLAZED BUTTERNUT SQUASH

1 (2-pound) butternut squash, peeled, cut in half lengthwise, and steamed
½ cup firmly packed brown sugar
½ teaspoon ground cinnamon
¼ teaspoon ground nutmeg
¼ teaspoon salt
3 tablespoons butter or margarine, melted

Arrange squash in a lightly greased 12- x 8- x 2-inch baking dish; set aside.

Combine brown sugar, cinnamon, nutmeg, and salt. Sprinkle mixture over squash halves; drizzle melted butter over top. Bake, uncovered, at 400° for 20 minutes or until tender. Yield: 6 to 8 servings.

Cushaw Pudding in casserole, Orange-Glazed Acorn Squash, and Smith House Glazed Butternut Squash. Super versatile, the wintry ones.

Some early advertising cards relied on slapstick humor to attract attention and convey a message as in this late 1800s seed advertisement.

SPICED CUSHAW PUDDING

1 (6-pound) cushaw squash
1 cup butter or margarine, softened
1 cup sugar
1 cup firmly packed brown sugar
1 teaspoon ground cinnamon
1 teaspoon ground nutmeg
1 tablespoon grated orange rind
2 teaspoons grated lemon rind
½ cup evaporated milk
½ cup milk
1 egg, beaten
Additional ground cinnamon (optional)
Additional ground nutmeg (optional)

Cut squash in half lengthwise; remove seeds and any fibrous material from center of squash. Cut squash into smaller pieces and place in a shallow baking dish; cover tightly. Bake at 350° for 1 hour and 15 minutes or until tender.

Remove squash from baking dish. Remove pulp from squash; discard skin. Mash pulp well using a fork. Drain thoroughly.

Combine mashed squash, butter, sugar, 1 teaspoon cinnamon, 1 teaspoon nutmeg, and rind in a large Dutch oven. Cook over medium heat 45 minutes or until thickened, stirring frequently. Add milk and egg, stirring well. Cook 10 minutes, stirring frequently.

Spoon squash mixture into twelve lightly greased 6-ounce custard cups. Sprinkle with additional spices, if desired. Bake at 325° for 20 minutes. Yield: 12 servings.

CUSHAW PUDDING

1 (5½-pound) cushaw squash
3 eggs, beaten
½ cup firmly packed brown sugar
2 tablespoons butter or margarine, melted
1 teaspoon vanilla extract
½ teaspoon pumpkin pie spice
¾ cup flaked coconut, toasted
3 tablespoons firmly packed brown sugar

Cut squash in half lengthwise; remove seeds and any fibrous material from center of squash. Cut squash into smaller pieces and place in a shallow baking dish; cover tightly. Bake at 350° for 1 hour and 15 minutes or until tender.

Remove squash from baking dish. Remove pulp from squash; discard skin. Mash pulp well using a fork. Drain thoroughly.

Combine mashed squash, eggs, ½ cup brown sugar, butter, vanilla, and pumpkin pie spice; mix well. Spoon mixture into a well-greased 2-quart casserole. Combine coconut and 3 tablespoons brown sugar; sprinkle evenly over top of casserole. Bake, uncovered, at 350° for 45 minutes. Yield: 10 to 12 servings.

TOMATOES

HOW TO PREPARE FRESH TOMATOES

2 medium-size tomatoes
1 tablespoon plus 1 teaspoon
    butter or margarine
Salt and pepper

To Clean: Although tomatoes may be served with the peeling, many people prefer them without the skin. To peel tomatoes, prepare a pan of boiling water. Impale a tomato through the stem end on a cooking fork, and dip into the water for 30 seconds. The skin can then be easily pulled off and discarded leaving a smooth surface.

If preferred, rub the surface of the tomato with the back of a knife. The skin may then be pared away with ease. Remove stem end with the tip of a sharp knife, leaving a funnel-shaped cut. Cut as directed in recipe. *Note:* Green tomatoes do not require peeling.

To Broil: Cut tomatoes in half, and place in a shallow baking dish. Place 1 teaspoon butter on each half; sprinkle with salt and pepper. Broil 5 minutes or until tomatoes are thoroughly heated. Yield: 4 servings.

Other Cooking Methods: Bake; fry; simmer.

Serving Suggestions: Tomatoes may be served with any of the following: Basil Vinegar, Chive Vinegar, French Dressing, Homemade Mayonnaise, Mayonnaise Dressing, or any sour cream sauce.

The Center for Southern Folklore

A photograph by Eudora Welty, one of the most acclaimed of Southern writers, who learned photography while working for the W.P.A. in her native Mississippi.

Men harvesting tomatoes, southeast Florida, c.1900.

SAUTÉED RICE AND TOMATOES

⅔ cup uncooked regular rice
¼ cup vegetable oil
1⅓ cups water
½ cup chopped onion
¼ cup bacon drippings
2 large tomatoes, peeled and chopped
1 teaspoon salt
½ teaspoon pepper

Cook rice in oil in a small cast-iron skillet, stirring frequently, until rice is lightly browned. Add water, and bring to a boil. Reduce heat; cover and simmer 20 minutes or until rice is tender. Set aside.

Sauté onion in bacon drippings until tender. Add tomatoes, salt, and pepper; bring to a boil. Reduce heat; cover and simmer 15 minutes. Add rice; stir well. Yield: 4 servings.

Tomato Stacks, filled with everything good. Invite someone nice for lunch.

TOMATO STACKS

3 large firm tomatoes, peeled
6 slices bread
6 slices bacon
1 medium-size green pepper, chopped
1 medium onion, chopped
½ teaspoon salt
¾ cup (3 ounces) shredded Cheddar cheese

Cut each tomato in half crosswise, and set aside.

Cut each bread slice with a 3½-inch cookie cutter. Toast bread rounds on each side, and set aside.

Cook bacon in a large skillet until crisp; drain well, reserving 2 tablespoons bacon drippings in skillet. Crumble bacon, and set aside.

Sauté green pepper and onion in reserved drippings until tender. Stir in salt.

Place toast rounds on a baking sheet. Top each toast round with a tomato half, sautéed mixture, cheese, and crumbled bacon. Broil until cheese melts. Yield: 6 servings.

SEASONED BAKED TOMATOES

8 medium-size firm tomatoes
2 cups soft breadcrumbs
2 tablespoons butter or margarine, melted
2 teaspoons chopped fresh parsley
1 teaspoon salt
¼ teaspoon pepper
1 teaspoon dried whole basil
Fresh basil leaves (optional)

Remove stems from tomatoes, and cut a ¼-inch slice from the top of each. Scoop out pulp, leaving shells intact. Set pulp aside. Invert tomato shells on paper towels to drain; set aside.

Press reserved pulp through a food mill or sieve. Combine pulp, breadcrumbs, butter, parsley, salt, pepper, and 1 teaspoon basil; mix well.

Spoon mixture into prepared tomato shells. Place tomatoes in a greased 8-inch square baking dish. Bake at 350° for 15 minutes. Garnish with fresh basil leaves, if desired, before serving. Yield: 8 servings.

TOMATOES BROWN

6 large tomatoes, peeled and quartered
1 small onion, chopped
¾ cup firmly packed brown sugar
1 cup soft breadcrumbs
½ teaspoon salt
⅛ teaspoon pepper

Place all ingredients in a small Dutch oven; bring to a boil. Reduce heat; cover and simmer 3 hours, stirring occasionally. Yield: 4 servings.

SUMMERTIME STEWED TOMATOES

10 medium tomatoes, peeled
1½ cups sugar
2 tablespoons butter or margarine
1 tablespoon lemon juice
½ teaspoon salt
¼ teaspoon dried whole basil
1 tablespoon chopped fresh parsley
2 slices bread, crust removed and cut into 2-inch strips

Combine tomatoes, sugar, butter, lemon juice, salt, and basil in a large saucepan. Bring to a boil. Reduce heat, and simmer 2½ hours or until mixture is thickened. Stir in parsley.

Spoon tomato mixture into a 1½-quart casserole. Top with bread strips. Bake, uncovered, at 350° for 20 minutes or until bread strips are browned. Yield: 6 servings.

FRIED RED TOMATOES

8 slices bacon
12 slices bread
1 cup all-purpose flour
1 teaspoon salt
½ teaspoon pepper
4 large firm tomatoes, peeled and cut into ½-inch slices
Sugar

Cook bacon in a large skillet until crisp; drain well. Crumble and set aside. Reserve drippings in skillet.

Cut each bread slice with a 3½-inch cookie cutter. Toast bread rounds on each side, and set aside.

Combine flour, salt, and pepper; mix well. Dredge 12 of the largest tomato slices in flour mixture; reserve smaller tomato slices for other uses.

Heat reserved drippings over medium heat; add dredged tomato slices, and cook until golden brown, turning once. Sprinkle sugar evenly over slices.

Place fried tomatoes on toast rounds, and sprinkle with bacon. Serve immediately. Yield: 12 servings.

Kentucky girl with profitable canning project, 1915.

The Filson Club, Louisville

Credit for introducing the tomato to the kitchens of Williamsburg belongs to Dr. John de Sequeyra, a physician who had arrived in the colony around 1745. He recommended eating tomatoes to prolong life and possibly (if eaten in sufficient quantities) even to attain immortality. He served on the board of the Public Hospital for the Insane from 1773 until mortality overtook him in 1796. Gradually, more people tried and liked tomatoes, but it was not until the advent of the metal can (1810) that they came into general use.

PAN-FRIED GREEN TOMATOES

½ cup all-purpose
  flour
½ teaspoon salt
¼ teaspoon pepper
2 large green tomatoes,
  cut into ½-inch
  slices
¼ cup butter or margarine
2 tablespoons plus 2
  teaspoons brown sugar,
  divided

Combine flour, salt, and pepper; stir well. Dredge tomato slices in flour mixture.

Melt butter in a large skillet. Fry tomato slices on one side until browned. Remove from skillet, and place in a 13- x 9- x 2-inch baking dish, browned side down.

Top each tomato slice with 1 teaspoon brown sugar. Broil 3 inches from heat 5 minutes or until browned and bubbly. Yield: 4 servings.

GREEN TOMATO CASSEROLE

4 medium-size green
  tomatoes, cut into
  ¼-inch slices
1 teaspoon sugar
1 teaspoon salt
½ teaspoon pepper
2 cups soft breadcrumbs
1 cup (4 ounces) shredded
  sharp Cheddar
  cheese
1 tablespoon butter or
  margarine, softened

Arrange one layer of tomato slices in the bottom of a lightly greased 1½-quart casserole. Combine sugar, salt, and pepper; mix well. Sprinkle tomatoes with about one-third each of sugar mixture, breadcrumbs, and cheese. Repeat layers, omitting cheese from top layer.

Dot butter over top of casserole. Cover and bake at 400° for 1 hour. Add remaining cheese. Bake, uncovered, 5 minutes or until cheese melts. Yield: 4 to 6 servings.

Fried Tomatoes with Gravy; biscuits fill out the meal.

FRIED TOMATOES WITH GRAVY

4 medium-size green
  tomatoes, cut into ¼-inch
  slices
2 eggs, beaten
1½ cups fine, dry
  breadcrumbs
½ cup bacon drippings
3 tablespoons all-purpose
  flour
2 cups milk
1 tablespoon prepared brown
  mustard
¾ teaspoon salt
¼ teaspoon pepper

Dip tomato slices in egg; dredge in breadcrumbs. Fry the tomato slices in hot bacon drippings in a large skillet until browned, turning once. Drain well on paper towels. Arrange on serving platter; set aside and keep warm.

Reserve bacon drippings in skillet. Add flour, stirring until smooth. Cook 1 minute, stirring constantly. Gradually add milk; cook over medium heat, stirring constantly, until thickened and bubbly. Stir in mustard, salt, and pepper. Spoon gravy over tomatoes to serve. Yield: 8 servings.

TURNIPS

HOW TO PREPARE FRESH TURNIPS

4 medium turnips
3 tablespoons butter or
   margarine, softened
½ teaspoon salt
¼ teaspoon pepper

To Clean: Turnips must be peeled before cooking. Scrub and peel thin layers. Cut in thin slices or cubes as directed in recipe.

To Boil: Cut turnips into ¼-inch cubes. Place in a saucepan, and cover with water; bring to a boil. Cook 15 minutes or until turnips are tender; drain. Mash, if desired. Season with butter, salt, and pepper. Yield: 4 to 6 servings.

Other Cooking Methods: Bake; deep-fry; steam.

Serving Suggestions: Turnips may be served with any of the following: Almond Butter, Dill Sauce, Drawn Butter, French Dressing, Horseradish Sauce, Lemon-Butter Sauce, Mustard Dip Sauce, or any sour cream or white sauce.

Baked Turnip Casserole may be the dish that converts the anti-turnip member of the family. Serve it as a hearty one-dish meal or take it to a pot-luck supper.

BROWNED TURNIPS

8 small turnips, peeled
  and sliced
2 tablespoons butter or
  margarine, melted
2 tablespoons sugar
½ teaspoon salt
¼ teaspoon pepper

Place turnips in a medium saucepan, and cover with water; bring to a boil. Cover and cook 10 minutes or until turnips are crisp-tender. Drain well.

Sauté cooked turnips in butter until evenly browned on one side. Sprinkle with sugar, salt, and pepper before turning to brown other side of turnips. Yield: 4 servings.

BAKED TURNIP CASSEROLE

10 slices bacon
1 cup chopped onion
1 clove garlic, minced
½ cup chopped green
  pepper
12 medium turnips, peeled,
  cooked, and mashed
2 egg yolks, beaten
1 (5.33-ounce) can
  evaporated milk
3 slices bread, toasted and
  crumbled
2 teaspoons chopped green
  onion tops
2 teaspoons chopped
  fresh parsley

Cook bacon in a large skillet until crisp; remove bacon, reserving 2 tablespoons bacon drippings in skillet. Crumble bacon, and set aside.

Sauté onion, garlic, and green pepper in reserved bacon drippings until tender. Stir in mashed turnips; cook over low heat 30 minutes. Remove from heat, and add yolks, milk, bread, green onion tops, and parsley; stir well.

Spoon mixture into a lightly greased 2-quart casserole, and sprinkle with reserved crumbled bacon. Bake, uncovered, at 350° for 30 minutes. Yield: 8 to 10 servings.

CREAMED TURNIPS

4 medium turnips, peeled and
  cubed
1 tablespoon sugar
1 tablespoon butter or
  margarine
1 tablespoon all-purpose flour
1 cup milk
½ teaspoon salt
¼ teaspoon white pepper
Chopped fresh parsley

Place turnips with water to cover in a medium saucepan; bring to a boil. Cover and cook 10 minutes. Add sugar; cook 5 minutes or until tender. Drain.

Melt butter in a heavy saucepan over low heat; add flour, stirring until smooth. Cook 1 minute, stirring constantly. Gradually add milk; cook over medium heat, stirring constantly, until thickened. Stir in salt, pepper, and turnips. Transfer to a warm serving dish; sprinkle with parsley and serve. Yield: 4 to 6 servings.

Mary Randolph, in *The Virginia Housewife*, recommended cooking small young turnips with 2 inches of the green tops left on. Old turnips should be peeled half an inch thick, she wrote, and the water changed when they are half-cooked. She did not mention sweetening them, but it has long been a Southern custom to serve turnips mashed and sweetened. P. Thornton, in his *Southern Gardener and Receipt Book,* 1845, says that "some roast turnips in a paper under embers, and eat them with sugar and butter." This writer gave a recipe for turnip bread, using turnips as we use potatoes in the loaf.

123

VEGETABLE COMBINATIONS

MIXED GARDEN VEGETABLES

6 slices bacon
6 medium-size green peppers, seeded and sliced into rings
8 medium tomatoes, peeled and sliced
4 medium onions, sliced
2 cups sliced fresh okra
½ teaspoon salt
⅛ teaspoon pepper
3 cups soft breadcrumbs

Cook bacon until crisp. Remove bacon, reserving bacon drippings. Crumble bacon, and set aside.

Pour 1 tablespoon bacon drippings into a 13- x 9- x 2-inch baking dish; tilt to coat surface. Layer green pepper rings, tomato slices, onion slices, and okra in baking dish. Sprinkle with salt and pepper.

Top vegetables with bacon and breadcrumbs; pour remaining drippings over breadcrumbs. Bake at 325° for 1 hour or until vegetables are tender. Yield: 10 servings.

SUMMER VEGETABLE CASSEROLE

¼ cup firmly packed brown sugar
2 teaspoons salt
½ teaspoon pepper
½ cup uncooked regular rice
1 small eggplant, peeled and sliced
1 large onion, sliced
3 medium-size yellow squash, sliced
3 medium zucchini, sliced
1 large green pepper, seeded and sliced
2 large tomatoes, peeled and sliced
2 tablespoons butter or margarine

Combine brown sugar, salt, and pepper. Set aside.

Place rice in bottom of a lightly greased 13- x 9- x 2-inch baking dish. Layer eggplant, onion, squash, zucchini, green pepper, and tomato in baking dish; sprinkle brown sugar mixture over each layer. Dot with butter. Cover tightly, and bake at 350° for 1½ hours or until rice and vegetables are tender. Yield: 10 to 12 servings.

FRESH VEGETABLE MEDLEY

6 slices bacon, diced
2 cups shelled fresh black-eyed peas (about 1 pound)
2 cups shelled fresh lima beans (about 1 pound)
3 cups water
1 teaspoon salt
½ teaspoon pepper
2½ cups fresh whole okra

Cook diced bacon in a large Dutch oven until crisp. Add black-eyed peas, lima beans, water, salt, and pepper; stir well. Cover and cook over medium heat 30 minutes. Add whole okra, and cook an additional 30 minutes or until okra is tender. Yield: 8 servings.

CUCUMBER COMBO

3 large onions, sliced
2 medium-size green peppers,
  seeded and chopped
2 cloves garlic, minced
½ cup butter or margarine
6 medium cucumbers, cut
  into ½-inch-thick slices
4 tomatoes, peeled and
  coarsely chopped
2 bay leaves
1 teaspoon salt
½ teaspoon pepper

Sauté onion, green pepper, and garlic in butter in a large Dutch oven until vegetables are crisp-tender. Stir in cucumber slices and tomatoes; add bay leaves, salt, and pepper. Stir well; cover and simmer 35 minutes. Remove bay leaves; discard. Serve immediately. Yield: 8 to 10 servings.

COLACHE

¼ cup chopped onion
1 large clove garlic, minced
2 tablespoons butter or
  margarine
4 medium-size yellow squash,
  cut into ⅛-inch slices
3 tablespoons all-purpose
  flour
2 cups fresh corn cut from
  cob
1 medium-size green pepper,
  seeded and coarsely
  chopped
2 teaspoons salt
⅛ teaspoon pepper
½ teaspoon ground oregano
½ teaspoon sugar
3 medium tomatoes, peeled
  and chopped
1 tablespoon capers (optional)

Sauté onion and garlic in butter in a heavy skillet over medium heat until tender.

Combine squash and flour; toss until coated. Add squash, corn, green pepper, salt, pepper, oregano, and sugar to sautéed vegetables in skillet; toss gently. Cover and cook over low heat 20 minutes. Add tomatoes and cook, uncovered, 10 minutes. Stir in capers, if desired. Yield: 6 to 8 servings.

Cucumber Combo is like a marvelous cooked salad.

VEGETABLE JAMBALAYA

6 slices bacon
1 pound fresh okra, cleaned
  and cut into ½-inch slices
2 medium onions, chopped
1 (14½-ounce) can whole
  tomatoes, drained
3 ears fresh corn, cut and
  scraped from cob
1 teaspoon salt

Cook bacon in a large skillet until crisp; drain on paper towels. Crumble and set aside, reserving drippings in skillet.

Sauté okra and onion in bacon drippings 5 to 7 minutes. Add tomatoes; cook over medium heat 5 minutes.

Add corn and salt to vegetable mixture; cook 5 minutes, stirring occasionally. Spoon vegetable mixture into a greased 10- x 6- x 2-inch baking dish; top with crumbled bacon.

Bake, uncovered, at 350° for 10 minutes or until thoroughly heated. Yield: 6 servings.

Ring Tum Diddy served on toast points and Vegetable Gumbo with rice.

GUMBO Z'HERBES

1 (2-pound) bunch mustard greens, cleaned
1 pound fresh spinach, cleaned
1 (½-pound) bunch watercress, cleaned
1 medium cabbage, shredded
4 cups water
2 tablespoons shortening
¼ pound ham hock, rinsed
½ cup chopped onion
¼ cup chopped green onion tops
¼ cup chopped fresh parsley
2 bay leaves
½ teaspoon dried whole thyme
3 tablespoons all-purpose flour, divided
2 teaspoons salt
½ teaspoon pepper
Dash of hot sauce

Place thoroughly washed greens on cutting board; using a sharp knife, cut greens into bite-size pieces. Place greens, shredded cabbage, and water in a large Dutch oven; bring to a boil. Reduce heat, cover and simmer 20 minutes. Remove greens mixture from Dutch oven and drain, reserving liquid. Set aside.

Melt shortening in a Dutch oven over medium heat; add ham hock, and cook until browned. Remove ham hock; set aside. Add greens mixture, onion, green onion tops, parsley, bay leaves, and thyme; cook over medium heat 3 minutes, stirring constantly. Stir in 2 tablespoons flour, salt, pepper, and hot sauce.

Add reserved ham hock and reserved liquid. Bring to a boil. Reduce heat, cover and simmer 1 hour.

Combine remaining flour and a small amount of water to form a smooth paste. Stir into greens mixture, and cook 1 minute. Yield: 12 servings.

VEGETABLE GUMBO

1 large onion, thinly sliced
¼ cup bacon drippings
6 medium tomatoes, peeled and sliced
4 cups fresh okra, cleaned and cut into ½-inch slices
1 cup boiling water
6 fresh mushrooms, sliced
1 clove garlic, minced
1 teaspoon salt
½ teaspoon pepper
Hot cooked rice

Sauté onion in drippings in a Dutch oven over medium heat until tender. Add tomatoes, okra, and water. Cover; cook over low heat 30 minutes, stirring occasionally. Add mushrooms, garlic, salt, and pepper. Cover; cook 30 minutes, stirring occasionally. Serve with rice. Yield: 8 to 10 servings.

RING TUM DIDDY

5 slices bacon
1 large green pepper,
   seeded and
   chopped
1 medium onion, chopped
2 cups fresh corn cut
   from cob
2 large tomatoes, peeled
   and chopped
½ teaspoon salt
¼ teaspoon pepper
1 cup (4 ounces) shredded
   Cheddar cheese
Toast points

Cook bacon in a large skillet until crisp; remove bacon, reserving drippings in skillet. Drain bacon well on paper towels; crumble and set aside.

Sauté green pepper and onion in reserved bacon drippings until tender. Add corn, tomatoes, salt, and pepper; cook over medium heat, 10 minutes, stirring frequently. Add cheese, and stir until cheese melts.

Top toast points with vegetable mixture. Serve immediately. Yield: 6 to 8 servings.

VEGETABLE HASH

6 medium-size green peppers,
   seeded and chopped
6 stalks celery, chopped
4 medium onions, chopped
¼ cup shortening
1 (28-ounce) can whole
   tomatoes, undrained
Hot cooked rice

Sauté green pepper, celery, and onion in shortening in a large Dutch oven until tender. Add tomatoes. Reduce heat and simmer 1 hour, uncovered, stirring occasionally. Serve over rice. Yield: 8 to 10 servings.

SUCCOTASH

4 slices bacon
1 medium onion, chopped
¼ cup chopped green pepper
2 cups shelled fresh lima
   beans (about 1 pound)
2 cups fresh corn cut from
   cob (about 4 ears)
2 tablespoons butter or
   margarine
⅛ teaspoon pepper
Fresh parsley sprigs

Cook bacon in a large skillet until crisp; remove bacon, reserving drippings in skillet.

Sauté onion and green pepper in bacon drippings until vegetables are tender. Add lima beans, corn, butter, and pepper; cover and cook over low heat 30 minutes or until vegetables are tender. Garnish with parsley. Yield: 4 to 6 servings.

Note: One (10-ounce) package frozen whole kernel corn, thawed, and one (10-ounce) package frozen baby lima beans, thawed, may be substituted for fresh vegetables.

POTATO MEDLEY

2 medium onions, sliced
3 tablespoons butter or
   margarine
2 medium tomatoes,
   peeled and sliced
2 pounds medium-size
   potatoes, peeled and
   cut into ⅛-inch
   slices
1 (10¾-ounce) can chicken
   broth, undiluted
1 teaspoon salt
½ teaspoon pepper
1 teaspoon paprika
Chopped fresh parsley
   (optional)

Sauté onion in butter in a Dutch oven until tender. Add tomatoes, potatoes, chicken broth, salt, pepper, and paprika. Cook over medium heat, uncovered, 30 minutes or until potatoes are tender, stirring occasionally. Sprinkle with parsley, if desired. Yield: 8 servings.

Balsam Apple and Vegetables, *an oil painting on canvas, by James Peale (1749-1831).*

Thomas Jefferson's Chartreuse of Vegetables: A showpiece he discovered in Paris that was immediately imitated by his circle of friends. Easier than it looks.

THOMAS JEFFERSON'S CHARTREUSE OF VEGETABLES

2½ pounds sweet potatoes
¼ cup whipping cream
½ teaspoon salt
Dash of pepper
1 pound fresh green beans
3 large carrots, scraped
Salt and pepper to taste
2 small zucchini, thinly
    sliced
2 medium potatoes or
    turnips, peeled and diced
¼ cup plus 2 tablespoons
    butter, melted
1 clove garlic, minced
1 cup fresh green peas
1½ cups (6 ounces) shredded
    Swiss cheese

Scrub sweet potatoes thoroughly; bake at 400° for 1 hour until potatoes yield slightly to pressure. Let cool to touch; peel and mash. Add whipping cream, ½ teaspoon salt, and dash of pepper; mix well, and set aside.

Break tips from green beans; remove strings. Wash in cold water and drain. Cut in 3½-inch lengths; set aside. Cut remaining pieces of beans into ¼-inch lengths. Set aside.

Cut carrots into 3½-inch lengths; slice into ¼-inch-thick strips. Set aside. Cut remaining pieces of carrots into ¼-inch-thick slices.

Place green beans in a steaming rack; steam over boiling water until crisp-tender. Immediately immerse in ice water to stop cooking. Drain well. Season with salt and pepper to taste; set aside. Repeat procedure with carrots, zucchini, and potatoes or turnips.

Combine butter and garlic; set aside.

Grease a 2-quart charlotte mold, and line bottom with waxed paper.

Arrange a layer of steamed vegetables and peas in an attractive pattern in bottom of charlotte mold. Spread one-fourth sweet potato mixture over vegetables. Place green beans and carrot sticks upright around side of mold, alternating beans and carrot sticks. Spoon one-fourth garlic butter over sweet potato mixture. Sprinkle with one-fourth Swiss cheese. Repeat layers three times.

Bake, uncovered, at 350° for 40 to 45 minutes. Cool in pan 10 minutes; invert onto serving platter. Serve warm. Yield: 8 servings.

FRESH VEGETABLE STEW

1 pound fresh green beans
1 cup shelled fresh
    black-eyed peas (about ½
    pound)
¼ cup bacon drippings
1 small cabbage, finely
    shredded
6 medium tomatoes, peeled
    and chopped
2 large potatoes, peeled and
    cubed
4 medium carrots, scraped
    and sliced
6 pods fresh okra, cut into
    ½-inch pieces
1 medium onion, chopped
1 hot red pepper pod, seeded
    and chopped
2 teaspoons salt
½ teaspoon pepper

Break tips from beans and remove strings; cut beans into 2-inch pieces. Wash thoroughly in cold water; drain. Place beans, peas, and drippings in a large Dutch oven. Add water to cover. Bring to a boil. Reduce heat; cook, uncovered, for 1 hour.

Add remaining ingredients; cover and cook over low heat 1 hour and 50 minutes or until vegetables are tender. Yield: 4 quarts.

ITALIAN-STYLE RATATOUILLE

3 medium onions, thinly
    sliced
2 medium-size green peppers,
    seeded and cut into ⅛-inch
    strips
2 stalks celery, cut in thin
    lengthwise strips
6 cloves garlic, minced
⅓ cup plus 2 tablespoons
    olive oil
2 medium eggplant, peeled
    and cubed
2 medium zucchini, thinly
    sliced
1 (16-ounce) can whole
    tomatoes, drained and
    coarsely chopped
2 teaspoons salt
½ teaspoon pepper
1 teaspoon dried whole
    oregano
½ teaspoon basil leaves
½ cup salad olives, chopped

Sauté onion, green pepper, celery, and garlic in oil in a large Dutch oven until vegetables are crisp-tender. Add eggplant and zucchini; cook 15 minutes, stirring occasionally. Add tomatoes, salt, pepper, oregano, and basil, stirring well; cover and cook 15 minutes. Sprinkle with olives before serving. Yield: 6 to 8 servings.

FINAL TOUCHES

To those of us in the South, some flavorful accompaniments to vegetables have become so automatic that a few of us might not even recognize the taste of greens without peppery vinegar sauce, or on occasion, a zesty herbed vinegar. To bring out the best in green beans, we have traditionally eaten green onions in season, and then sliced or chopped onions as both beans and onions matured. In winter, those onions are still our most reliable and appetizing topper for all our dried beans and peas. There is a very special sauce, a vegetable medley, that is considered a necessity down in Mason County, Texas. They spoon it all over black-eyed peas and beans, either green or dried; now, with that recipe included in our "Final Touches" chapter, we can all go and do likewise.

Southerners have never apologized for cooking their green beans "to death," but it is not widely known that, properly motivated, we can cook them as crunchy as the most sophisticated chef can and dress them in as many ways, from herb-buttered to hollandaised to amandined. It is just that we may want to cook them half a day with salt pork or ham hocks if we are alone with the home folks; and that is a preference that bears no relationship to ignorance.

Not unlike cooks in other parts of the country, Southerners have picked up on the healthful advantage of the crudité tray for parties. Cultured sour cream, not available many years ago, is the basis for many of our zippiest sauces and dips. For generations, we have doted on homemade mayonnaise and hollandaise dressings. With the electric blender to make these favorites foolproof and almost instantaneous, we probably use them more often now than our grandmothers did.

Nowadays, we may vary our vegetable routine by taking this leaf from the professional saucier's notebook: Instead of saucing a vegetable over the top, try placing the sauce on a serving dish and arrange the vegetable on the sauce. Picture: A golden mornay sauce, white cauliflower, drift of chopped parsley overall. Another show-off: Grandmother Flexner's Asparagus Sauce, pale yellow, *under* fresh asparagus, with strips of pimiento over the stems to make them into visual bundles. Eating with the eyes, we call it.

Bewildering array of fresh herbs photographed at Mordecai House, Raleigh, North Carolina. Think of an herb . . . spearmint, savory, tarragon, rose geranium, sage, marjoram, thyme, basil, sorrel, parsley, sage . . . they're all here, and more.

ALMOND BUTTER

3 tablespoons butter or
  margarine
1 (2-ounce) package slivered
  almonds

Melt butter in a skillet; sauté almonds in butter until golden brown. Yield: ½ cup.

TANGY BUTTER SAUCE

2 tablespoons butter or
  margarine
2 tablespoons olive oil
1½ teaspoons Worcestershire
  sauce
1 teaspoon prepared mustard
Red pepper to taste

Melt butter in a heavy saucepan over low heat; add remaining ingredients, stirring until well blended. Serve warm. Yield: about ⅓ cup.

DRAWN BUTTER

1 cup butter

Melt butter over low heat in a 1-quart saucepan without stirring. When completely melted, remove from heat; let stand so that the butter separates, allowing the milk solids to settle to the bottom.

Skim butter fat from the top, and reserve for another use. Place several layers of cheesecloth in a strainer, and strain the clear yellow liquid into a dish. Yield: about ½ cup.

LEMON-BUTTER SAUCE

2 tablespoons butter
2 tablespoons all-purpose
  flour
2 cups water
1 tablespoon chopped fresh
  parsley
1½ teaspoons lemon juice
¾ teaspoon salt
⅛ teaspoon pepper

Melt butter in a heavy saucepan over low heat; add flour, stirring until smooth. Cook 1 minute, stirring constantly. Gradually add water; cook over medium heat, stirring frequently, 20 minutes or until thickened and bubbly. Stir in parsley, lemon juice, salt, and pepper. Yield: about 1½ cups.

HORSERADISH SAUCE

2 tablespoons finely chopped
  onion
2½ tablespoons butter or
  margarine
2 egg yolks, beaten
1 cup whipping cream
2 tablespoons prepared
  horseradish

Sauté onion in butter in a heavy saucepan until tender. Strain butter and onion mixture through a sieve into beaten egg yolks. Add whipping cream; stir well. Cook yolk mixture in top of a double boiler over medium heat, stirring constantly, until thickened. Stir in horseradish; serve hot or cold. Yield: about 1 cup.

BASIC WHITE SAUCE

1 tablespoon butter or
  margarine
2 tablespoons all-purpose
  flour
1 cup milk
½ teaspoon salt
¼ teaspoon white pepper

Melt butter in a heavy saucepan over low heat; add flour, stirring with a wire whisk until smooth. Cook 1 minute, stirring constantly. Gradually add milk; cook over medium heat, stirring constantly, until thickened and bubbly. Stir in salt and pepper. Yield: 1 cup.

Note: For a thinner white sauce, delete 1 tablespoon flour, and for a thicker white sauce, add 1 tablespoon flour.

GRANDMOTHER FLEXNER'S ASPARAGUS SAUCE

3 tablespoons butter or
  margarine
2 tablespoons all-purpose
  flour
1 cup milk
2 egg yolks, beaten
2 tablespoons lemon juice
1 tablespoon sugar
¼ teaspoon salt
1 tablespoon whipping cream
Ground cinnamon

Melt butter in a heavy saucepan over low heat. Add flour; stir until smooth. Cook 1 minute; stir constantly. Gradually add milk; cook over medium heat, stirring constantly, until thickened and bubbly.

Combine egg yolks, lemon juice, sugar, and salt.

Gradually stir a small amount of hot milk mixture into egg mixture; add to remaining hot milk mixture, stirring constantly. Add whipping cream; blend well. Sprinkle with cinnamon. Yield: 1¼ cups.

CHEESE SAUCE

1 tablespoon butter or
  margarine
2 tablespoons all-purpose
  flour
¼ teaspoon salt
Dash of white pepper
1 cup milk
¾ cup (3 ounces) shredded
  sharp Cheddar cheese

Melt butter in a heavy saucepan over low heat; add flour, salt, and pepper, stirring until smooth. Cook 1 minute, stirring constantly. Gradually add milk; cook over medium heat, stirring constantly, until thickened. Add cheese; stir until cheese melts. Yield: 1¼ cups.

BLENDER HOLLANDAISE SAUCE

4 egg yolks
2 tablespoons lemon
  juice
¼ teaspoon salt
Dash of pepper
½ cup butter, melted

Combine egg yolks, lemon juice, salt, and pepper in container of an electric blender; process at high speed until thick and lemon colored.

Turn blender to low speed; add butter to yolk mixture in a slow, steady stream. Turn blender to high speed; process until thickened (about 30 seconds). Yield: ⅔ cup.

Late 1800s salad dressing advertisement.

HOLLANDAISE SAUCE SUPREME

4 egg yolks
½ cup butter, melted
¼ teaspoon salt
Dash of pepper
2 tablespoons lemon juice

Place egg yolks in top of a double boiler; beat until thick and lemon colored. Slowly add butter, salt, and pepper. Bring water to a boil. Reduce heat to low; cook, stirring constantly, until smooth and thickened.

Remove from heat; stir in lemon juice. Serve immediately. Yield: ⅔ cup.

MOCK HOLLANDAISE SAUCE

2 egg yolks
Thick White Sauce
3 tablespoons lemon juice
Dash of red pepper

Beat egg yolks; gradually stir about one-fourth of hot Thick White Sauce into egg yolks. Stir into remaining hot Thick White Sauce. Cook over medium heat 2 minutes, stirring constantly. Remove from heat; gradually add lemon juice, stirring well. Stir in pepper. Yield: 1¼ cups.

Thick White Sauce:

3 tablespoons butter or
  margarine
¼ cup all-purpose flour
1 cup milk
¼ teaspoon salt

Melt butter in a heavy saucepan over low heat; add flour, stirring until smooth. Cook 1 minute, stirring constantly. Gradually add milk; cook over medium heat, stirring constantly, until sauce is thickened and bubbly. Stir in salt. Yield: about 1 cup.

133

HOMEMADE MAYONNAISE

1 teaspoon salt
½ teaspoon dry mustard
¼ teaspoon paprika
Dash of red pepper
2 egg yolks
2 tablespoons vinegar
2 cups vegetable oil, divided
2 tablespoons lemon juice

Combine salt, mustard, paprika, and pepper in a deep, narrow bowl. Add egg yolks, and beat at high speed of an electric mixer until thickened. Add vinegar; beat well.

Add 1½ cups oil, 1 tablespoon at a time; beat at high speed until mixture begins to thicken. Add remaining ½ cup oil, alternately with lemon juice, 1 tablespoon at a time. Spoon into a glass or plastic container; cover and refrigerate. (Do not store mayonnaise in a metal container.) Yield: about 2 cups.

MAYONNAISE DRESSING

2 hard-cooked egg yolks
1 egg yolk
½ teaspoon prepared mustard
½ cup olive oil, divided
1 tablespoon lemon juice
2 teaspoons vinegar
½ teaspoon salt
Paprika

Combine cooked egg yolks and raw egg yolk; beat on medium speed of an electric mixer until smooth. Add mustard, beating well.

Add ¼ cup oil (1 drop at a time) to yolk mixture, beating constantly at medium speed. Add lemon juice, vinegar, and salt; beat well. Add remaining oil, 1 tablespoon at a time, making sure oil is thoroughly combined with egg yolk mixture before adding another tablespoon. Scrape bowl frequently.

Spoon Mayonnaise Dressing into a jar with tight-fitting lid; store in refrigerator. Garnish with paprika when serving. Yield: about ¾ cup.

BLENDER MAYONNAISE

1 egg
1 teaspoon salt
1 teaspoon dry mustard
¼ teaspoon paprika
Dash of red pepper
2 cups vegetable oil, divided
¼ cup vinegar
2 tablespoons lemon juice

Combine egg, salt, mustard, paprika, red pepper, and ½ cup oil in container of an electric blender; process at high speed until thickened. Slowly add ½ cup oil, blending well. Add vinegar and lemon juice; process until well blended. Slowly add remaining 1 cup oil, blending thoroughly. Yield: about 2 cups.

DILL SAUCE

1½ cups mayonnaise
1 (8-ounce) carton commercial sour cream
2 tablespoons olive oil
2 tablespoons lemon juice
1 teaspoon Worcestershire sauce
½ cup chopped fresh parsley
1 tablespoon dried dillweed
1 teaspoon garlic salt
1 teaspoon dry mustard
2 drops hot sauce

Combine all ingredients, mixing well. Chill thoroughly. Yield: 2½ cups.

FRENCH DRESSING

½ cup olive oil
2 tablespoons plus 2 teaspoons tarragon vinegar
2 cloves garlic, minced
½ teaspoon salt
¼ teaspoon white pepper

Combine all ingredients, mixing well. Cover and refrigerate 1 to 2 hours. Yield: ⅔ cup.

OIL AND LEMON SAUCE

¼ cup plus 2 tablespoons olive oil
¼ cup plus 2 tablespoons lemon juice
2 tablespoons chopped fresh parsley
2 cloves garlic, minced

Combine all ingredients in a jar. Cover tightly, and shake until mixture is well blended. Chill. Yield: ¾ cup.

MUSTARD DIP SAUCE

1 cup vinegar
2 (1.12-ounce) cans dry mustard
3 eggs, beaten
1 cup sugar

Combine vinegar and mustard; mix well. Cover and refrigerate overnight.

Add eggs and sugar to mustard mixture; stir well. Place mixture in a small saucepan; bring to a boil. Reduce heat, and simmer 10 minutes or until slightly thickened, stirring well. Serve hot or cold. Yield: 2 cups.

VEGETABLE HOT SAUCE

20 jalapeño peppers
5 small tomatoes, finely chopped
2 small onions, finely chopped
3 cloves garlic, minced

Place peppers and water to cover in a small saucepan; cover and bring to a boil. Cook 5 minutes; drain and cool. Remove seeds from peppers, and finely chop peppers.

Combine chopped peppers, tomatoes, onion, and garlic; mix well. Cover and refrigerate overnight to blend flavors. Stir sauce well before serving. Yield: about 3 cups.

Note: Vegetable Hot Sauce can be refrigerated up to 2 weeks.

SOUR CREAM DRESSING

¼ cup vinegar
¼ cup water
1 egg yolk
2 tablespoons sugar
1 tablespoon all-purpose flour
1 tablespoon butter or
  margarine
½ teaspoon dry mustard
Dash of paprika
1 (8-ounce) carton
  commercial sour cream

Combine all ingredients except sour cream in top of double boiler, stirring well. Bring water to a boil. Reduce heat to low; cook, stirring gently, until thickened. Cool slightly, and add sour cream; stir well. Chill. Yield: 1⅓ cups.

SWEET-AND-SOUR DRESSING

1 egg, beaten
1 tablespoon bacon drippings
¼ cup sugar
¼ cup vinegar
¼ cup commercial sour
  cream

Combine egg and drippings in a small ceramic saucepan; beat well with a wire whisk. Place over medium heat; cook until thickened slightly, beating constantly with wire whisk.

Dissolve sugar in vinegar; gradually add to egg mixture. Cook over low heat, stirring constantly, until thickened. Cool slightly, and fold in sour cream. Yield: about ¾ cup.

CHIVE BLOSSOM VINEGAR

¾ quart chive blossoms
About 1 quart white vinegar,
  scalded

Pack chive blossoms into a sterilized quart jar. Fill jar with vinegar, leaving a ½-inch headspace. Cover with a metal lid; screw band tight. Let stand at least 2 weeks. Strain and rebottle vinegar. Yield: 1 quart.

FRESH TOMATO SAUCE

2 cloves garlic, minced
2 tablespoons butter or
  margarine
2 cups peeled, seeded,
  chopped tomatoes
¼ cup chopped fresh parsley
¼ cup finely chopped cooked
  ham
¼ teaspoon salt
Dash of pepper

Sauté garlic in butter until tender. Stir in tomatoes and parsley. Simmer 40 minutes or until thickened, stirring occasionally. Stir in ham, salt, and pepper. Yield: about 2 cups.

HOT PEPPER SAUCE

7 small hot peppers (red or
  green)
¾ cup vinegar
¼ teaspoon pickling salt

Wash peppers, and pack solidly into a sterilized pint-size jar. Combine vinegar and salt in a small saucepan; stir well. Bring to a boil. Remove from heat, and immediately pour over peppers, leaving a ½-inch headspace. Cover at once with a metal lid, and screw metal band tight. Refrigerate for at least 1 hour before serving. (May be kept refrigerated up to 1 year). Yield: 1 pint.

Mason County Relish (front) shown with Basil Vinegar and Chive Vinegar.

CHIVE VINEGAR

¾ cup chopped chives
1 quart white vinegar, scalded

Place chives in a sterilized quart jar. Fill jar with vinegar, leaving a ½-inch headspace. Cover with a metal lid, and screw band tight. Let stand at least 2 weeks. Strain and rebottle vinegar. Yield: 1 quart.

BASIL VINEGAR

¾ cup dried whole basil
1 quart apple cider vinegar, scalded

Place basil in a sterilized quart jar. Fill jar with vinegar, leaving a ½-inch headspace. Cover with a metal lid, and screw band tight. Let stand at least 2 weeks. Strain and rebottle vinegar. Yield: 1 quart.

MASON COUNTY RELISH

1 medium onion, chopped
1 small green pepper, seeded and chopped
¾ teaspoon salt, divided
2 medium tomatoes, peeled and chopped
¼ cup vinegar
1 tablespoon sugar
⅛ teaspoon pepper

Combine onion, green pepper, and ½ teaspoon salt in a medium saucepan; add water to cover. Bring to a boil; cover and reduce heat. Simmer 10 minutes. Drain thoroughly.

Combine cooked vegetables and tomatoes; mix well. Add remaining salt, vinegar, sugar, and pepper, stirring well. Cover and refrigerate at least 1 hour. Yield: about 2 cups.

TART CELERY RELISH

1½ cups thinly sliced celery
½ cup finely chopped cabbage
½ cup chopped green pepper
¼ cup chopped pimiento
¼ cup sifted powdered sugar
¼ cup apple cider vinegar
1 teaspoon salt
½ teaspoon dry mustard

Combine all ingredients; mix well, and store in a tightly covered container. Chill at least 2 hours. Drain off liquid before serving. Yield: about 2½ cups.

CREAM MINT SPREAD

1 (8-ounce) package cream cheese, softened
½ cup cream-style cottage cheese
½ teaspoon dried whole garden mint, crushed

Beat cream cheese until smooth. Add cottage cheese and mint, mixing well. Spoon mixture into a covered container; chill at least 12 hours. Yield: about 1½ cups.

HERB SPREAD

4 (3-ounce) packages cream cheese, softened
2 tablespoons butter or margarine, softened
1 tablespoon chopped chives
2 tablespoons dried dillweed
1 teaspoon chopped fresh parsley
¼ teaspoon garlic powder

Combine all ingredients, mixing well. Spoon mixture into a covered container; chill at least 1 hour or until ready to use. Yield: about 1½ cups.

HERB BUTTER

1 cup butter, softened
1 tablespoon chopped chives
1 tablespoon chopped fresh parsley
½ teaspoon dried whole marjoram
½ teaspoon dried whole basil
1 teaspoon lemon juice

Combine all ingredients, and beat until light and fluffy. Store mixture in a covered container in refrigerator until ready to use. Yield: 1 cup.

TARRAGON HERB BUTTER

1 cup butter, softened
½ teaspoon dried whole basil
½ teaspoon ground thyme
½ teaspoon dried whole tarragon
½ teaspoon chopped chives
½ teaspoon dried whole rosemary, crushed

Combine all ingredients, and beat until light and fluffy. Store mixture in a covered container in refrigerator until ready to use. Yield: 1 cup.

The smiling gardener in this ad from a 1919 seed catalogue encouraged a war-weary nation to grow food.

THE HOPE OF THE NATION

PETER HENDERSON & Co.

GLOSSARY

Bake: To cook in an oven, with or without liquid, with or without a cover, as directed in a given recipe.

Boil: To cook in water at 212° F. The term is used loosely, as most of the foods we "boil" could more accurately be called simmered. A few, such as corn on the cob and spaghetti, should be cooked at a "hard" or "full rolling" boil. But usually we mean that a food is brought to a boil, the heat reduced, and then simmered until done.

Braise: To cook slowly in moist heat in a covered utensil.

Deep-fry: To cook in oil deep enough to cover food, heated to temperature indicated in a recipe.

Fry: To cook at medium high in shortening or other fat in skillet or Dutch oven, using amount of fat indicated in recipe.

Poêle: To cook food in its own liquid. A French term meaning "to sweat"; we may call it smother. A heavy saucepan is buttered generously, the vegetable added, and waxed paper is pressed on top of the food. Covered closely with a lid, the pan is placed on high for a few moments to make steam form inside pan. Heat is reduced to below simmering, and vegetable is cooked tender.

Sauté: To fry lightly over medium heat in a small amount of fat in a shallow, open pan, stirring frequently.

Simmer: To cook in liquid at or below the boiling point with little or no visible movement of the food or cooking liquid. Simmering is preferred to boiling in most cases as the food cooks without the rolling motion which tends to break up tender vegetables.

Steam: To cook on a rack placed in a cooking vessel with water or other liquid poured under rack, not touching food. Pan is covered with lid.

Stew: To boil slowly or with simmering heat. We usually reserve the term for those long-cooking Southern vegetables such as greens and snap beans.

Stir-fry: To cook freshly cut food Chinese-style in a small amount of oil in a wok or skillet. Cook over medium high heat, stirring often, until vegetables are crisp-tender.

Stir-fry/Steam: A combination cooking method in which the food is first stir-fried, and then liquid (usually chicken broth) is added and the lid placed on wok or skillet. We follow stir-fry with steam in the case of hard vegetables, such as sliced carrots, when further tenderizing is desired.

INDEX

ACKNOWLEDGMENTS

Asparagus and Peas with Egg Sauce, Fresh Asparagus in Bacon Rings, Cauliflower Maître d'Hotel, Split Green Beans courtesy of the Home Economics Club, Dallas, Texas.

Asparagus Meringue, Fried Fresh Asparagus first appeared in *Presbyterian Cook Book*, published 1934.

Asparagus Vinaigrette, Bacon Hominy, Onions au Gratin, Boiled Cabbage, Squash Drumsticks adapted from *Famous Kentucky Recipes*, compiled by Cabbage Patch Circle, ©1952.

Asparagus with Mushrooms and Cream Sauce, Broccoli Baked with Cheese Sauce, Broiled Stuffed Mushrooms, Browned Turnips, Parsnip Cakes, Stuffed Green Peppers, Tomatoes Brown, Zucchini Stuffed with Tomatoes adapted from *Maryland's Way* by Mrs. Lewis R. Andrews and Mrs. J. Reaney Kelley, ©1966. By permission of The Hammond-Harwood House Association, Annapolis, Maryland.

Aunt Sivie's Green Crowder Peas courtesy of Mrs. Ed Brown, Pine Bluff, Arkansas.

aked Okra courtesy of Mrs. Edwin O'Brien, Lafayette, Louisiana. First appeared in *First - You Make A Roux* by Lafayette Museum Association, Lafayette, Louisiana, ©1954.

aked Stuffed Mushrooms adapted from *The Gasparilla Cookbook* by The Junior League of Tampa, ©1961. By permission of The Junior League of Tampa, Florida.

aked Turnip Casserole, Louisiana Mustard Greens, Mustard Greens and Turnips adapted from *Talk About Good* by The Junior League of Lafayette, Inc. By permission of The Junior League of Lafayette, Louisiana.

aked Vidalia Onions, Baked Vidalia Onions in Sherried Cream Sauce, Crunchy Asparagus with Vidalia Onions, Stuffed Vidalia Onions courtesy of The Vidalia Chamber of Commerce, Vidalia, Georgia.

aked Zucchini and Tomatoes, Shaker Lemon-Glazed Carrots, Stuffed Zucchini adapted from *We Make You Kindly Welcome* by Elizabeth C. Kremer, ©1970. By permission of Shakertown at Pleasant Hill, Harrodsburg, Kentucky.

arbecued Green Beans adapted from *Southern Cooking* by Mrs. S.R. Dull, ©1941. By permission of Grosset and Dunlap, New York.

asil Vinegar, Chive Vinegar, Creamed Green Peas and Potatoes, Salsify Bisque, Scalloped Salsify adapted from *Welcome Back to Pleasant Hill* by Elizabeth C. Kremer, ©1977. By permission of Shakertown at Pleasant Hill, Harrodsburg, Kentucky.

roccoli Parmesan, Green Onion Pie adapted from *Julie Benell's Favorite Recipes* by Julie Benell, ©1956. By permission of Doubleday, Inc., New York.

arrot Balls adapted from *Recipes from the Old South* by Martha Meade, ©1961. By permission of Holt, Rinehart, and Winston, New York.

auliflower Duchesse adapted from *Southern Sideboards* by The Junior League of Jackson, ©1978. By permission of The Junior League of Jackson, Mississippi.

elery and Pecan Casserole, Summertime Stewed Tomatoes adapted from *Huntsville Heritage*, compiled by The Grace Club Auxiliary, ©1967. By permission of The Grace Club Auxiliary, Huntsville, Alabama.

elery Colle adapted from *Melrose Plantation Cookbook* by Francois Mignon and Clementine Hunter, ©1978. By permission of Mrs. R.B. Williams, Natchitoches, Louisiana.

hayote Squash, Mississippi Style, Cucumber Combo, Cushaw Pudding adapted from *The Jackson Cookbook*, compiled by the Symphony League of Jackson. By permission of the Symphony League of Jackson, Mississippi.

hili Hominy, German Sauerkraut, Wine Sauerkraut adapted from *Guten Appetit!*, compiled by the Sophienburg Memorial Association, ©1978. By permission of the Sophienburg Museum, New Braunfels, Texas.

hive Blossom Vinegar, Dill Sauce, Herb Butter, Herb Spread, Green Beans Tarragon, Tarragon Herb Butter adapted from *A Source of Much Pleasure*, edited by Virginia Phillips Holz. By permission of The Mordecai Square Historical Society, Raleigh, North Carolina.

olache, Florida Sautéed Cucumbers, Florida Simmered Celery, Green Peppers Stuffed with Fresh Vegetables adapted from *Jane Nickerson's Florida Cookbook* by Jane Nickerson, ©1973. By permission of University Presses of Florida, Gainesville, Florida.

ream Mint Spread courtesy of Marsha Presnell-Sennette, gardener for Mordecai House, Raleigh, North Carolina.

reole Black-Eyed Peas, Passion Peas, Southern-Cooked Black-Eyed Peas courtesy of the Black-Eyed Pea Jamboree, Athens, Texas. By permission of Mohrle-Francis Advertising, Dallas, Texas.

reole Lima Beans adapted from *The Fredericksburg Home Kitchen Cook Book*, published by The Fredericksburg Home Kitchen Cook Book Central Committee, ©1957.

ried Lima Beans with Sausage, Fried Tomatoes with Gravy adapted from *Plantation Recipes* by Lessie Bowers, ©1959. By permission of Robert Speller and Sons Publishers, Inc., New York.

randmother Flexner's Asparagus Sauce, Louis Smith's Southern Fried Onions adapted from *Out of Kentucky Kitchens* by Marion Flexner, ©1949. By permission of Franklin Watts, Inc., ©1981.

reen Peas and Drop Dumplings courtesy of Frances Edwards, Tampa, Florida.

eritage material for Fried Pumpkin or Squash Blossoms adapted from *Idle Hens Don't Lay* by The Cookbook Committe, Parents and Friends of Woodlawn Academy, Chatham, Virginia.

asyone's Red Beans and Sausage courtesy of Mr. James D. Lasyone, Lasyone's Restaurant, Natchitoches, Louisiana.

aque Chou courtesy of Mrs. Donald Labbe, Lafayette, Louisiana. First appeared in *First - You Make a Roux* by Lafayette Museum Association, Lafayette, Louisiana, ©1954.

ason County Relish courtesy of the Vedder family, Mason, Texas.

enger Hotel Spinach Loaf courtesy of Ann Elizabeth Bush, Menger Hotel, McKinney, Texas.

kra Pilâu adapted from *Savannah Sampler* by Margaret Wayt DeBolt, ©1978. By permission of The Donning Company Publishers, Norfolk, Virginia.

ed Cabbage with Apples adapted from *Square House Museum Cookbook*, ©1973. By permission of Carson County Square House Museum, Panhandle, Texas.

mith House Glazed Butternut Squash, Smith House Squash Casserole courtesy of The Smith House, Dahlonega, Georgia.

tuffed Banana Peppers adapted from *Acadiana Profile's Cajun Cooking*, edited by Trent Angers and Sue McDonough, ©1980. By permission of Angers Publishing Corporation, Lafayette, Louisiana.

ummer Vegetable Casserole adapted from *The Bush Family Cookbook*. Courtesy of Mrs. Bob Morris, Dallas.

ext on Beans adapted from *Mrs. Blackwell's Heart of Texas Cookbook* by Louise B. Dillow and Deenie B. Carver. By permission of Corona Publishing Company, San Antonio, Texas.

ext on Cauliflower adapted from *Two Hundred Years of New Orleans Cooking* by Natalie V. Scott, New Orleans, Louisiana. Published by Jonathan Cape and Harrison Smith.

homas Jefferson's Chartreuse of Vegetables adapted from *Thomas Jefferson's Cook Book*, edited by Marie Kimball, ©1979. By permission of University Press of Virginia, Charlottesville, Virginia.

THE Magazine For You
if You Share Our Interest
in the South.

SOUTHERN LIVING
features articles to help make
life for you and your
family more comfortable,
more stimulating, more fun...

SOUTHERN LIVING is about your home and how to make a more attractive, more convenient, more comfortable place to live. Each issue brings you dozens of decorating and remodeling ideas you can adapt to your own surroundings.

SOUTHERN LIVING is about gardening and landscaping and how to make the outside of your home just as attractive as the inside. In addition to gardening features, you'll find a monthly garden calendar pinpointing what to plant and when, plus a "Letters to our Garden Editor" section to answer your own particular questions.

SOUTHERN LIVING is about good food and entertaining, with recipes and menu ideas that are sure to delight your family and friends. You'll discover recipes with a Southern accent from some of the South's superlative cooks.

SOUTHERN LIVING is about travel and just plain fun. Every new issue offers an information-packed monthly calendar of special events and happenings throughout the South, plus features on the many fascinating places of interest the South has to offer.

To find out how you can receive SOUTHERN LIVING every month, simply write to: SOUTHERN LIVING, P. O. Box C-119, Birmingham, AL 35283.